The Compact Guide to
World Religions

The Compact Guide to
World
Religions

LION

Sean O'Callaghan

Copyright © 2010 Sean O'Callaghan
This edition copyright © 2010 Lion Hudson

The author asserts the moral right
to be identified as the author of this work

A Lion Book
an imprint of
Lion Hudson plc
Wilkinson House, Jordan Hill Road,
Oxford OX2 8DR, England
www.lionhudson.com

ISBN 978 0 7459 5318 2

Distributed by:
UK: Marston Book Services, PO Box 269, Abingdon, Oxon, OX14 4YN
USA: Trafalgar Square Publishing, 814 N. Franklin Street, Chicago, IL 60610
USA Christian Market: Kregel Publications, PO Box 2607, Grand Rapids, MI 49501

First edition 2010
10 9 8 7 6 5 4 3 2 1 0

Acknowledgments
Bible quotations taken from the *Holy Bible, New International Version*, copyright ©
1973, 1978, 1984 International Bible Society. Used by permission of Zondervan and
Hodder & Stoughton Limited. All rights reserved. The 'NIV' and 'New International
Version' trademarks are registered in the United States Patent and Trademark Office
by International Bible Society. Use of either trademark requires the permission of
International Bible Society. UK trademark number 1448790.
Quotations from the Qur'an are taken from Khalidi, Tarif (translator), *Penguin Classics:
The Qur'an*, Penguin, 2008.

A catalogue record for this book is available
from the British Library

Typeset in 9.5/11 Bodoni Svty Two ITC TT
Printed and bound in China

Contents

Introduction

The death of religion has long been forecast and the phenomenon of religious faith continues to confound its critics and doomsayers. If one were to take any serious daily newspaper anywhere in the world and cut from it every story that had some connection with faith, there would at the end of the exercise be very little of the newspaper remaining. Matters of faith and belief impinge on and pervade the geo-political scene, particularly in the Middle East and central Asia. US foreign policy is greatly influenced by the religious and geo-political ramifications that result from the location of the state of Israel, and conflicts all over the globe have their roots in religious diversity and argument. The anticipated secularization of the world, particularly the Western world, has not taken place, and many are now speaking about the re-sacralization of society, where sacred and religious themes are mediated to a receptive audience through the influence of film, books and cyberspace, as well as through new religious movements.

One only has to visit the 'Mind, body and spirit' section of any major bookshop to encounter a wide variety of books offering

An Israeli soldier is seen on top of a tank at a staging area near Israel's border with Gaza.

a bewildering array of spiritual paths and solutions. Supernatural storylines abound on our TV screens and in our cinemas. People worldwide, even in nations where religious belief is persecuted, still search for spiritual meaning in either the traditionally established religions of the world, or in new spiritualities that are emerging all the time to fill the gaps left in societies by what many see as the inabilities of the older world religions to adapt to changing spiritual paradigms.

It was the German scholar Friedrich Max Müller (1823–1900) who pioneered the academic study of religion as we know it today. In the intervening years between his initial research and our own time, the study of religion in universities and other places of learning has grown rather than diminished and interest in religious belief and spirituality has continued to rise. The reasons for this sustained engagement with matters of belief – even in a world where science has long been taken by so many to have displaced the need for God and where religion might, as a result of human progress, have been viewed as a reservoir of superstitious belief belonging to a bygone era – are many. Where religion lies at the root of conflict and political and social development, the student of religion perhaps is seeking to understand the historical and the sociological reasons behind the various issues. A particular nation may be fully understood only by insight into the religious history that has formed its psyche. Globalization is a major factor in maintaining the study of world faiths, since world travel, the influence

of the mass media and the role of the internet have combined to cast as forever redundant the notion that other beliefs belong to other lands and cultures. Now, on our neighbourhood streets, members of a multiplicity of faith communities live in close proximity to each other and attend very diverse places of worship. For many people the study of religion is an exercise in trying to understand their own faith more deeply or the faith of a member of their family. It may even be that some want to challenge their own beliefs at the deepest possible level and engage in a root-and-branch evaluation of their own belief system, regardless of whether that system is theistic or not.

The Study of Religion

The study of religion, however, is really a cumulative outcome of a number of disciplines that bring different insights into matters of faith. This is only to be expected, since religion is a human activity. This may be a point of contention for some who believe that the doctrines and revelations of their own religion are divinely inspired and given directly by God; but, no matter how much one might believe in such a divinely mediated transmission of faith, there needs to be a recognition that faith is lived out within the context of human society and is influenced by the limitations and the potentialities of human, earthly realities. The existence of religion across the whole of human society and culture has led many thinkers to propose that there is a common factor at work within the human psyche and that a distinction can be drawn between 'faith' and 'faiths': 'faith' is understood as a universal facet of the human condition, where human beings are creatures who are predisposed to belief; 'faiths' are the outward expressions of this inner belief and are subject in their development to substantial variations owing to differing geographical, political, climatic, philosophical and psychological conditions.

Neurotheology, an emerging branch of theology that seeks to understand religion in terms of the human mind and brain chemistry, proposes that religious experiences are no more than the result of events within the human brain itself, events that can be caused by various stimuli, both internal and external. Whatever the truth of neurotheology's assumptions, it is one more reminder that no matter how divinely inspired a religious path claims to be, it is still 'lived out' in fallible human beings. Over the past century and a half, scholars of religion have examined religion using different disciplines, each of which teases out important strands:

◆ *Phenomenology* tries to view religions objectively, without making value judgments about a religion's truth claims. It tries to understand what the religion means to the believer and locate the essence of the religion, distinguishing this from the rituals and outward phenomena while not ignoring these aspects. An important factor in the study of the phenomenology of religion is the development of critical faculties that produce judgment not influenced by bias; or at least the recognition that one's interpretations may be open to bias and the willingness to allow for this.

◆ *Anthropological* approaches to religion arise out of the study of human life and culture. Religion is viewed as a fact of human culture and the culture itself is the focus of research so that the origins and practice of religion can be better understood.

◆ *Sociological studies of religion* view religious ideas and practices as being inspired and formed by something within the relevant society. They analyze how religious activity relates back to the society in which it is rooted and look at how religious expressions in a society relate to each other. They examine the influence of religion on the society as well as that of society on religion. They recognize that religious activity can arise and develop along certain lines because of social processes, or that society can be changed and formed by religious world-views.

◆ *The philosophy of religion* explores the philosophical assumptions that lie behind or underpin belief. Philosophical approaches to the study of religion look at reasons for certain world-views and also reasons for belief in the existence of God, if the religion is theist.

◆ *The psychology of religion* examines the role of the emotions and feeling in religious practice. It enquires about the human needs that might encourage a

highly complex and multi-layered 'faiths' as they attempt to make sense of what they intuitively feel is beyond themselves and their physical world.

The Guide provides a snapshot of the major world religions and an overview of each that looks not only at origins, doctrines and teachings, but also at how the religions are expressed in daily life, through festivals, in the family and in society in general. The Guide tries to root religion in real, daily existence and seeks to present the faiths as living, dynamic, spiritual systems which need constantly to adapt themselves to changes within their relevant cultures and societies.

William James, c.1890.
American philosopher
and psychologist.

person to become religious or to seek solace and meaning in religious belief. This approach was first introduced in a serious way by the US American psychologist William James (1842–1910), who wrote *The Varieties of Religious Experience*.

This Compact Guide offers the reader a compendium of essential facts as an aid to a better practical and basic understanding of the religious practices and core beliefs of the adherents of the twelve faith paths covered. Such an understanding may in turn lead to a greater insight into what inspires human beings – throughout the globe – to express 'faith' through these

Christianity

History and Development

The name 'Christianity' is derived from the Greek title 'Christos', which was ascribed to a first-century Jewish man, Jesus of Nazareth, by his early followers. The term was used to mean 'the messiah' or 'the anointed one' – that is, the saviour figure of Jewish apocalyptic teaching.

As well as developing from Judaism and retaining much of its symbolism and theology (the Hebrew scriptures – known by Christians as the Old Testament – are used extensively by those who regard their faith as the fulfilment of Jewish prophecy and teaching), Christianity owes a great deal to first-century Greek culture, thought, and philosophy. While its roots were in Judaism, Christianity was rapidly influenced by streams of thought in the Greco-Roman world in which it grew. Both its Jewish character and the Greco-Roman environment to which it was quickly transplanted enabled it to expand swiftly throughout the whole Mediterranean world. From its inception it became a missionary faith: expansion was a policy and a strategy.

Birth of the church

Christianity began to emerge as a system of faith very shortly after the death of Jesus. Initially, Jesus' core followers numbered twelve and this 'inner circle' became known as the 'twelve apostles'. By the time of Jesus' crucifixion, the disciples had been together for almost three years and the death of their leader dealt a severe blow to what up until then had looked like a reform movement within first-century Judaism in the area around Galilee.

However, the event known as the resurrection of Jesus turned what had seemed to be a disastrous blow for the

Size With approximately 2.1 billion followers, the largest of the world religions.

Founder Jesus of Nazareth, called Jesus Christ.

Location Originating in the early first century CE around Galilee (in modern-day Israel) and now worldwide.

followers of Jesus into a triumph over death and failure, and transformed them into the vibrant community that is described in the Acts of the Apostles, especially in chapters 1–3.

Accounts of the resurrection and subsequent events are to be found in all four gospels (Matthew 28:1–20; Mark 16:1–20; Luke 24:1–49; John 20:1–21:25). On visiting his tomb some days after his death, the followers of Jesus found it to be empty. The gospels and the Acts of the Apostles teach that the resurrected Jesus appeared to the disciples on several occasions after his resurrection. Paul, writing in 1 Corinthians 15:6, adds that having appeared to Peter and then to the twelve apostles, Jesus also appeared in his resurrected body to more than 500 others. In Luke 24:44–47, the resurrected Jesus explains to the disciples that the Jewish scriptures had foretold not only his death, but also his rising from the dead.

It is impossible to overestimate the impact the news of the resurrection had on the disciples. Following the ascension of Jesus to heaven, forty days after the resurrection (Acts 1:1–11), the disciples gathered in

Fresco of *The Last Supper*, 1495–97, by Leonardo da Vinci (1452–1519).

an upper room in Jerusalem on the Jewish feast of Pentecost, where Acts 2 describes them as receiving power from the Holy Spirit and being empowered to preach the message of Jesus. This empowerment led to the followers of Jesus boldly meeting in the Temple on a daily basis (Acts 2:44–47). Upon doing so, they grew in strength and numbers into the first Christian community, until the persecution described in Acts 8 caused them to have to spread out throughout the region, bringing the Christian message with them and advancing the growth of the early Christian church. As a result of persecution, the followers of Jesus ceased from meeting in Jewish synagogues and began to meet in each others' homes.

The community of Christian believers is known as the 'church', and this church quickly spread to Asia Minor (encompassing modern-day Turkey among other areas). It was in this region that many local churches were established.

The Apostle Paul, 1520, by Vittore Carpaccio, c.1455/65–1526.

Paul of Tarsus

The early Christian believers were severely persecuted for their faith and one of the foremost of their persecutors was a learned Pharisee from the city of Tarsus, a member of a strict sect within Judaism noted for meticulous observance of the Jewish law. He was also a Roman citizen. However, after a dramatic experience while journeying to the city of Damascus, he joined the followers of Jesus, who knew him as Paul.

He was a well-educated man, able to speak Aramaic and Greek. He was expert in matters of Jewish teaching and also Greek learning. Paul was to be a crucial figure in the establishment of Christianity in the Greek-speaking world, well able to bridge the cultural, linguistic and religious gaps. He was instrumental in the setting up of churches in the major population centres of Asia Minor and was also a very good strategist. Many of his letters to the churches which he founded, or over which he had some authority, are extant and contained within the New Testament. These give a valuable insight into the early evolution of the churches and the challenges facing them. They also act as valuable sources for the development of Christian theology.

Developing Christian thought

As the church grew in number and influence, many questions about belief arose. This brought about disputes and controversies and many different splits and movements. Early Christianity very much found itself amongst an array of other faiths and it had to define itself and what it believed in. Notable scholars, known later as 'the church fathers', helped to develop Christian theological thinking amidst the many debates about the exact nature and role of Jesus. As has been noted, Christianity was strongly influenced by Greek thought, as was Judaism before it. The introduction of Christianity to the Greek-speaking world brought about the incorporation of Greek ideas and concepts into the faith. The Egyptian city of Alexandria was one place where Christianity particularly encountered Greek thought. In that city two very influential Christian thinkers, Clement (150–213 CE) and Origen (180–253 CE), were instrumental in interpreting Christian thinking in terms that were in line with the thought of the Greek philosopher Plato. This establishment of a clear relationship

Right: Obverse of a coin from the era of Constantine the Great who ruled 306–337 CE.

Far right: Martin Luther nails the ninety-five theses to the door of Wittenberg Cathedral 31 October 1517.
An 1872 painting by Ferdinand Pauwels (1830–1904).

with Greek philosophers further strengthened the position of Christianity, especially in intellectual circles.

Church and empire

In 313 CE the emperor Constantine decreed that Christianity become the state religion of the Roman empire. As a result, Christianity became strongly organized and institutionalized. It also became politicized. It was now even more important to define the beliefs of the church, and many councils were held at which theologians debated at length the divinity or otherwise of Jesus and the nature of God. Many streams of thought and theories about Jesus were regarded as heretical. The Arian controversy (named after Arius, c. 250–336 CE) resulted in a council in 325 CE, which settled on the belief that Christ had not – as a creature might be – been made by God, but rather was 'begotten' of God the Father and was the Son of God. Another group viewed as heretics, the Adoptionists, argued that Jesus was entirely human and had merely been adopted as a son by God.

These confusions about the exact nature of Jesus were settled at the Council of Chalcedon in 451 CE, where a formula was agreed to the effect that Christ was both fully God and fully man. After the fall of the Roman empire and the rise of the Eastern capital of the empire, Constantinople, the

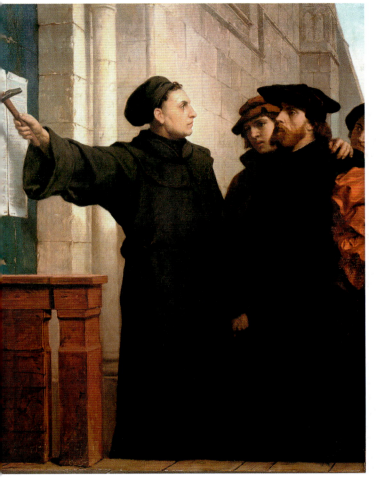

church in the West and the church in the East began to develop in different ways, adopting variant practices and doctrines. In the West the papacy grew in power, both spiritually and politically. The Eastern church was run by a number of patriarchs, based in major centres and regions. In 1054, the spiritual and political disputes between both sides reached a climax, and a schism, or split, formally occurred.

The crusades

The highly controversial religious conflicts known as 'the crusades' took place against the backdrop of the Muslim occupation of Jerusalem. In 1095 Pope Urban II initiated the first crusade with the object of placing 'Christian sites in the Holy Land' under Christian control. The crusades continued well into the thirteenth century and were the cause of intense hostility and bloodshed.

The term was also applied to papal campaigns against Christian groups regarded as heretics, such as the Albigensian Crusade, begun in 1209, which resulted in the slaughter of many Cathars in southern France.

The Reformation

In the fifteenth century deep divisions emerged between the Roman Catholic Church, led by the pope, and Christians throughout Europe rebelling against the centralized control of a church dominated by a clerical class. The Renaissance of the fourteenth century had encouraged Christians to focus on the Bible as a means of personal revelation; church authority was severely questioned. The need for human mediators, such as the pope and priests, came under scrutiny. In the sixteenth century many reform movements arose in a period known as 'the Reformation'.

The Reformation took place particularly

in England, Scotland, Germany, France, Switzerland and the Netherlands. In 1517 the German monk Martin Luther (1483–1546) challenged church authority by pinning to the door of the church in Wittenberg ninety-five issues for debate. Luther fought against practices in the church which he considered to be corrupt and unbiblical, such as the selling of indulgences, or pardons, for sins committed. In Switzerland, John Calvin (1509–64) preached against the practices of the Roman Catholic Church, centring his movement on the city of Geneva. In England, Henry VIII (1491–1547) desired to divorce his wife and clashed with the pope. As a result Henry declared himself, not the pope, to be head of the church in England. Henry's daughter Elizabeth (1533–1603) became queen in 1558 and carried reforms to greater lengths.

Protestantism
The various reform movements often organized themselves in churches which are known by the term 'Protestant'. They rejected what they saw as unnecessary ornamentation and concentrated on keeping services simple and in the ordinary language of the people, not in Latin as in the case of the Roman Catholic Church. The Roman Catholic Church responded with its own internal reformation, particularly formulated by the Council of Trent (1545–63). However, the splits had taken place and a number of Protestant groups went on to develop their own church structures and theologies. These major divisions still characterize the Christian church worldwide today.

Challenge and diversity
The Christian church continued to face challenges in the following centuries from the increasing role which secularism was to play in human society. The eighteenth-century Enlightenment emphasized the authority of the human being and the power of the human mind to think for itself without the need for God. Many philosophers argued against the existence of God and the notion that God was just a creation of the human mind gained ground. However, Christianity has been adept at engaging with such thought and Christian missionary activity has continued to enable the churches to gain considerable ground in an ever more secular and scientific age. While Christian churches have declined in influence in the West, many – particularly Protestant churches of an evangelical nature – are growing with great speed in areas of Africa, Asia, and South America. Evangelical churches focus on personal response to the Christian message and encourage a change of heart and changed lives. They place the Bible and the message of the death of Jesus as a sacrifice for sin at the centre of their Christian theology.

Founder and Significant Figures

Jesus of Nazareth never used the term 'Christianity'. He was, however, its inspiration.

Jesus of Nazareth
Jesus was born in Bethlehem, just south of Jerusalem in the region of Judea. The story of his birth, which is credited with miraculous signs, is told at the beginning

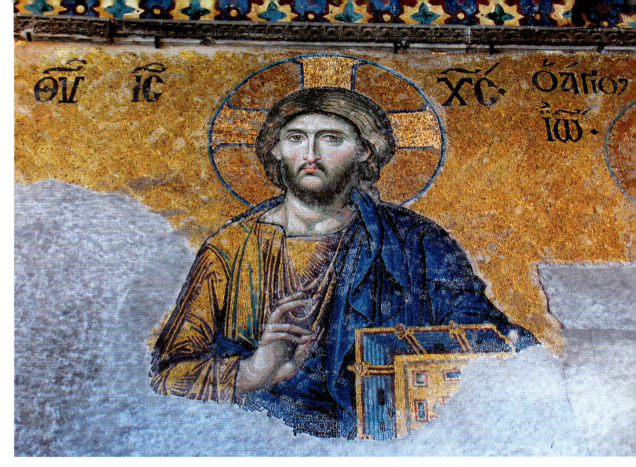

of the Gospel of Luke. The precise year is uncertain. Recent research suggests 5 or 6 BCE.

The four Gospels are our main source for information on the life of Jesus. Little is known of his youth. He is portrayed as coming from the house of David, the royal line. This and other indicators in the Gospels present him as a 'messiah' figure. The

messiah was the one whom Jews expected to come to save them from their oppression and captivity. At this time, they were under the rule of the Roman empire. Jesus, then, was born into a society which was in some political turmoil, with great resentment against the governing authorities.

The mother of Jesus was named Mary. His father was Joseph, although the Gospels

Depiction of Christ in the Deësis mosaic, from the Church of Holy Wisdom, Istanbul, Turkey.

claim that Jesus was not conceived in the normal biological way, so Joseph was not his natural father. Luke 1:30–33 explains that an angel appeared to Mary to tell her she would conceive miraculously by the power of the Holy Spirit and not by any human agency. Jesus grew up in the town of Nazareth, 110 km (68 miles) north of Jerusalem in the area of Galilee, a region known to be a hotbed of unrest and anti-Roman feeling.

The ministry of Jesus

At the age of thirty Jesus began his ministry of preaching, being baptized in the River Jordan by his cousin John, known as John the Baptist. In the Gospels John has the role of forerunner to Jesus, preparing the way for his ministry. This was marked by many miracles, such as healing the sick and even raising the dead. Exorcisms, or the driving out of evil spirits, feature large in the accounts.

One of the main themes of Jesus' preaching was the coming of the kingdom of God, where the reign and influence of God would be extended. The gospel was the 'good news' of this. 'The kingdom of God is near. Repent and believe the good news!' (Mark 1:15).

Jesus clashed very often with the Jewish spiritual authorities, especially the Pharisees, a strict Jewish group. However, he also gathered many followers around him, including quite a few women and the group of twelve who are recorded as being more trusted than others. He and his followers travelled around and Jesus preached his message. At other times he taught his closest disciples things that could not be shared with everyone. Jesus mixed with all levels of society and his friendship with those considered unacceptable by the authorities created considerable conflict. He counted among his friends tax collectors, who were despised by the populace, and people who were generally regarded as sinners. He also challenged strict Jewish rules, arguing that rigidity and compassion could not always go together. He spoke constantly about the love of God and taught that relationship with this God was not about keeping outward rules, but about a change of heart and of lifestyle.

Opposition to Jesus' message

His message made him many enemies and the Jewish leaders conspired to have him arrested, charged with blasphemy by the Jewish courts, and with provocation to stir up trouble with Rome by the Roman authorities. This arrest took place after a meal known as 'the Last Supper', during which Jesus shared bread and wine with his disciples. Christians remember this meal in their churches when they take wafers of bread and wine from a cup, believing that the bread and wine represent or become the body and blood of Jesus. He was crucified on a cross, an image which has since come to be the defining symbol of Christianity. The Gospels claim that on the third day after his death, Jesus rose from the tomb, as he had promised to do when he was alive, and appeared to his disciples and to others. Christians believe that, with this resurrection from the dead, Jesus defeated the power of death and paved the way for

Christians to also live spiritually for eternity. Jesus is therefore characterized as being no ordinary man, but a prophet, a miracle worker, a spiritual revolutionary, and the Son of God.

Peter and Paul

The apostles were entrusted with passing on the message of Jesus. The most influential apostle of all – as portrayed in the Acts of the Apostles, a book of the New Testament – is Paul, who, as it has been noted, took Christianity out into a larger, regional context.

Another major figure among the apostles, regarded by many as a rival to Paul, was Peter. Peter was very close to Jesus and was considered to be the chief of the apostles. According to Roman Catholic teaching, he went on to become the first pope. Originally called Simon, Peter took his name from the Greek word for a 'rock', *petra* or *petros*, which was in turn the Greek equivalent of the Aramaic *kepha*. Peter took the leading role amongst the apostles on the death of Jesus and became a key figure in the Jerusalem church.

Branches of Christianity

Over the centuries the main branches of Christianity have split into several denominations, each of which will also have its own sub-sections. The divisions between the Eastern and Western churches and the aftermath of the Reformation have resulted in a wide variety of approaches in theology, church government, style of worship, place of worship and world-view.

The Beatitudes

The Beatitudes[1] are found in both the Gospels of Matthew (5:1–12) and Luke (6:20–26). The word 'beatitude' is the English translation of the Greek term *makarios*, which was the word used to describe the state of someone who had attained life's ideal. *Makarios* is not the usual word in Greek for 'happiness' but is often used by philosophers and poets of the Greek Classical period to denote a state of 'blessedness', a state where, in spite of appearances, the person blessed is getting the best out of life and is actually storing up reward in another life. The Beatitudes are understood as a series of blessings that follow from a right attitude in life.

Matthew writes of eight beatitudes, Luke of four. Luke, however, also has four 'woes' and Matthew none. Matthew is clearer about the spiritual nature of the blessing involved. For example, Luke writes, "Blessed are you who are poor, for yours is the kingdom of God" (Luke 6:20). Matthew expands on this and writes, "Blessed are the poor in spirit, for theirs is the kingdom of heaven" (Matthew 5:3). The 'woes' of Luke are visited on the rich, the satisfied and the complacent who abuse their power in this life and forfeit any hope of reward in the next (Luke 6:24–26).

The eight beatitudes of Matthew are:

- ◆ Blessed are the poor in spirit, for theirs is the kingdom of heaven.
- ◆ Blessed are those who mourn, for they will be comforted.
- ◆ Blessed are the meek, for they will inherit the earth.
- ◆ Blessed are those who hunger and thirst for righteousness, for they will be filled.
- ◆ Blessed are the merciful, for they will be shown mercy.
- ◆ Blessed are the pure in heart, for they will see God.
- ◆ Blessed are the peacemakers, for they will be called sons of God.
- ◆ Blessed are those who are persecuted because of righteousness, for theirs is the kingdom of heaven.

Roman Catholicism

While Protestant churches have developed many denominations and sub-denominations, the Roman Catholic Church itself, though not free from debate and controversy, has largely maintained its unity under the authority of the pope, who governs from Rome.

Right: A priest offers Eucharist in Paris, France.

Below: Pope Benedict XVI delivers the 'Urbi et Orbi' message from the central Loggia of St Peter's Basilica at the Vatican.

The role of the papacy

The Roman Catholic Church is the largest of the Christian churches and its members number close to one billion. Its governmental structure is much centralized, with the pope, who is also the bishop of Rome, presiding over a complex structure known as the Roman Curia. It is the Curia that runs the Roman Catholic Church worldwide and it can be understood as a kind of 'civil service'. The Roman Catholic Church believes itself to be directly in

continuity with the church founded by the first bishop of Rome, Peter the apostle. The pope is known as the 'Successor to Peter' and Roman Catholics believe he carries a direct authority because of that. In 1870 the pope was declared by the cardinals, who with the pope administer the church, to be infallible. This means that when he speaks with the authority of Peter, as his direct successor, he is incapable of making an error when defining a matter of faith and morals. To do this, he must speak *ex* *cathedra* (from the chair of authority) and not just as part of general teaching.

The sacraments

Roman Catholics believe in seven *sacraments* (actions or rituals that mediate the grace of God to an individual). These are:

Baptism	When a child or an adult is initiated into the faith.
Confirmation	Where the promises made at baptism (usually made on behalf of a baby by parents and godparents) are acknowledged and 'confirmed'. Confirmation entails the receiving of the power of the Holy Spirit, so adult candidates who have affirmed their own baptismal promises also receive confirmation.
Holy Communion	Receiving bread and wine, usually, but not exclusively, during the Roman Catholic mass. Communion can also be received in the home by those who are ill, or at special ceremonies where a priest may not be available to say mass but where non-ordained members of the church can still distribute the bread and the wine. Roman Catholics believe that the bread and wine are changed into the actual body and blood of Jesus as a result of the words spoken during the mass by the priest.
Ordination of a man to the priesthood of the church	Roman Catholics believe that when a man is ordained into the priesthood, he receives special powers from God. He receives the authority to absolve sins on behalf of God and he can perform the mass where bread and wine are turned into the body and blood of Christ. Only men can be ordained in the Roman Catholic Church and the ordination must be performed by a bishop.
Penance	When an individual confesses sins and failings to a priest so that forgiveness can be attained.
Marriage	The Roman Catholic Church regards marriage as a sacred union between man and woman.
Extreme unction	Also known as the 'last rites', extreme unction entails the anointing of the sick and dying person or the person in danger of death. It is meant to comfort the dying and prepare them for death.

The Russian Orthodox Patriarch of Moscow and All Russia, Kirill I, holds an Orthodox Easter service in Moscow, in Christ the Saviour Cathedral.

The mass

The church service at which Holy Communion is celebrated is the central and most important ceremony of the Roman Catholic Church and all Catholics are required to attend mass either on Sunday or the evening before. Mary, the mother of Jesus, has an important role within Roman Catholic theology, where she is given the title 'Mother of God'. She features

prominently in Roman Catholic prayers and practices.

East and West

In 1054 a formal split, or 'schism', occurred between the Eastern and Western churches. This split came about because of doctrinal differences, mainly about whether the Holy Spirit had its source in the Father and the Son, or in the Father alone, but through the Son. The clause in dispute was known as the *Filioque* clause. There were also many differences in perspective between East and West, particularly in how each viewed the condition of humanity and in how each believed God could be approached or related to. They also held differing political views and opinions as to how the church should be governed. The Eastern churches did not accept the pope of Rome as the supreme authority over them, although some Eastern churches did remain in communion with Rome, but by mutual agreement followed their own customs and rites.

There are about 250 million Eastern Orthodox believers worldwide. They are ruled by patriarchs, who are religious leaders. These patriarchs do not have any overall authority over Orthodoxy and many are based in the historic centres of Eastern Christendom, such as Constantinople, Alexandria, Antioch and Jerusalem.

Eastern Orthodoxy places a strong emphasis on mysticism and its liturgy is usually very visual, very rich and involves all the senses, through the use of incense and sacred oils. Icons or sacred images are also widely used.

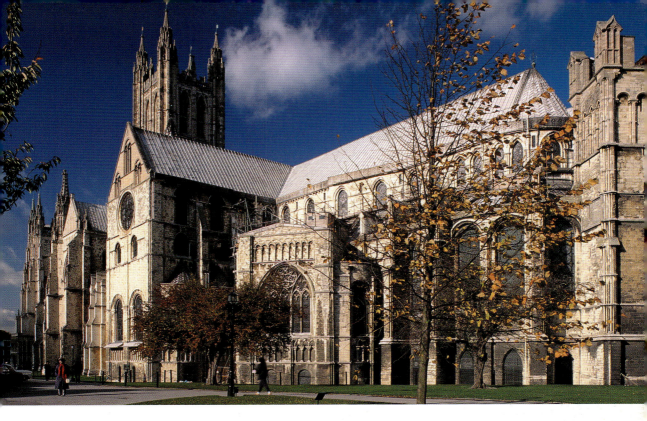

Canterbury Cathedral in the UK.

Protestant and Reformed churches

The Reformation, in particular, gave rise to a large number of churches in the 'Protestant' tradition.

Anglicanism

The Anglican church developed during the Reformation. It regards itself as Catholic, though not Roman Catholic – rather, it believes itself to be Reformed. It claims continuity with the historic Catholic church, but does not subject itself to Rome or to papal authority. This position came about when Henry VIII of England rejected papal supremacy and declared himself 'Supreme Head of the Church'. The Queen of England still holds the title 'Supreme Governor of the Church of England' and the church is presided over by the Archbishop of Canterbury, who is regarded as the 'first among equals' in relation to the other churches of the Anglican communion worldwide. Churches in many

25

lands regard themselves as members of the wider Anglican communion, but answer to their own bishops and archbishops, rather than to Canterbury. The Anglican church tends to embrace a variety of approaches to belief. Parts of it, particularly the Anglo-Catholic wing, are very close to Roman Catholicism in belief and style, while other areas are much closer in style of worship and belief, though not in governmental structure, to the Reformed churches that rejected sacramentalism and priestly or episcopal church government.

Methodism

Methodism grew out of an evangelical revival that spread across the UK and North America in the eighteenth century. John Wesley (1703–91) and his brother Charles (1707–88) were its prime movers and both were Anglican clergymen. Methodism grew out of Anglicanism, but maintained a distinctively evangelical character. Preaching and hymn-singing remain important features of its worship.

Lutheranism

The Protestant churches of Germany and Scandinavia follow styles of worship and belief systems that have their origins in the teachings of the reformer Martin Luther. There are about 70 million Lutherans worldwide. Central to Lutheran teaching is the chief Reformation tenet that justification before God is by faith alone, not by works.

Free Churches

Other Protestant groupings grew out of what might be called a more thoroughgoing reformation process, where church government was radically altered and where less formal forms of worship were encouraged. Often, this means that these churches do not follow a set liturgy, although liturgy may be used on occasions such as weddings and funerals. These may be known as 'Free churches'.

Many of the Free churches are independent organizations with no central authority, but they may be joined to similar groupings under an 'umbrella' agreement. This is particularly true for churches of a Pentecostal or charismatic nature. These churches believe in freedom of worship style and often reject meeting in traditional church buildings. They have a fluid leadership structure. Other Free churches may be less fluid and adopt more rigid styles of worship and government, but will be free of central authority and able to make autonomous decisions for their own congregations, while subscribing to some common guidelines.

Baptists

These belong to a worldwide group of believers who share a conviction that only adults should be baptized. This is also called *believers' baptism*. It is a very influential denomination in North America.

Society of Friends (Quakers)

This denomination was founded in the seventeenth century and its followers espouse a very simple form of worship,

devoid of any liturgy or adornment. Quakers do not follow a central creed, nor do they have priests, ministers or sacraments. Meetings are held in silence until a member feels 'moved by the spirit' to speak. The group was founded by George Fox (1624–91).

Pentecostal and charismatic churches
These follow a very loosely organized form of worship. Pentecostals trace their roots to an evangelical revival in the late nineteenth and early twentieth century in the USA, which quickly spread worldwide. Today, Pentecostals are making considerable progress in Latin America and Africa, where their use of music and large gatherings, coupled with an emphasis on the power of the Holy Spirit and on the ability of the Holy Spirit to work in a visible way in the world, draws a large following. It has also gained considerable ground in North America, large parts of Europe, especially the UK, and also Australia and New Zealand. The charismatic movement grew out of the Pentecostal movement

Brigflatts, a Quaker meeting house, near Sedbergh, Cumbria, UK.

The gifts of the Holy Spirit

Within charismatic and Pentecostal churches, a lot of emphasis is put on the ability of God, through the Holy Spirit, to intervene directly and dramatically in peoples' lives today. This can involve healing, deliverance from evil forces, or specific divine guidance. A central feature of Pentecostal worship is the use of music and also of praying in tongues, a form of ecstatic utterance, where the believer claims to be speaking in a different language, inspired by the Holy Spirit. Pentecostal practice has been widely adopted across a number of denominations, although in some areas it is treated with great suspicion and is regarded as deviant behaviour or emotionalism. Its style of worship, particularly its music, has been very influential even in churches that reject its emphasis on the gifts of the Holy Spirit.

and tended initially to manifest itself as a Pentecostal-type movement within the historic traditional churches, for example within Roman Catholicism and mainstream Protestantism. Many churches prefer to describe themselves as 'charismatic' rather than Pentecostal as they believe that use of this term best reflects subtle changes in approach and theology that have developed since the initial Pentecostal revival.

Members of the Bay Ridge Christian Center Pentecostal Church pray during a two-hour church service in Brooklyn, New York City.

Sacred Writings

The sacred scriptures of Christianity are contained within one book – the Bible – which is made up of many other books. It can be best understood as a collection of books, which taken together encompass a wide array of genres. It is divided into two main sections.

◆ The Old Testament (sometimes known as the Hebrew Bible) includes the entire Jewish scriptures.

◆ The New Testament is that part of the Bible which contains writings composed since the time of Jesus Christ.

Jesus himself wrote nothing of which we are aware. The earliest Christians had only the Jewish scriptures and it took some time for a body of Christian work to be developed. Even then, the Christian church continued to use the Old Testament as it regarded itself as being in continuity with the teachings and worship of the God of the Jewish scriptures.

The New Testament

The New Testament is made up of twenty-seven books containing many different categories and styles of writing. In fact, many other writings were composed during the early Christian period, but not all of these were accepted as being 'inspired' or carrying divine authority. Therefore, they were not included in the 'canon' – the officially recognized collection of scriptures.

The books of the New Testament

The four Gospels	The four Gospels, ascribed to Matthew, Mark, Luke, and John, tell the story of the life of Jesus from different perspectives. Matthew, Mark, and Luke – because they tend to be more in agreement with each other – are known as the 'synoptic' Gospels. One theory is that Mark was written first and was used as a basis for Matthew and Luke; Matthew added his material to support a Jewish viewpoint, while Luke was concerned to give Jesus a wider context, especially for the non-Jewish or 'Gentile' world. Another theory supposes a separate common source known as Q (from the German, *Quelle*, meaning 'source'). The dates given for the writing of the Gospels vary widely, but many scholars tend to opt for a date after 70 CE. In general, John's Gospel is thought to date from 90 CE.
The book of Acts	The Acts of the Apostles is the second part of the Gospel of Luke, separated from Luke in the compilation of the books so that the Gospels could be grouped together. Acts follows the four Gospels and tells the story of the development of the early church. It focuses strongly on events at Jerusalem following the death of Jesus and on the roles of both Peter and Paul.
The letters of Paul, John, Peter, James and Jude	The letters of Paul, John, Peter, James and Jude are known as 'epistles'. Thirteen of these, the great majority, were ascribed to Paul and are written either to individuals or to churches.
The letter to the Hebrews	The letter to the Hebrews is of disputed authorship, with Paul being traditionally, though certainly not universally, credited with its composition.
The book of Revelation (or Apocalypse)	The final book of the New Testament, the book of Revelation, is written in a visionary and apocalyptic style.

The Dead Sea Scrolls

The term 'Dead Sea Scrolls'[2] refers to texts found in caves along the north-west shore of the Dead Sea between the years 1947 and 1956. Not all of the scrolls discovered are related to each other. The first scrolls were discovered by accident in a cave near the Wadi Qumran. The texts appear to belong to communities based in the area of Qumran. They were probably copied in the closing centuries BCE or the early years CE up to 70 CE, the date of the siege of Jerusalem. It is possible that the scrolls were hidden to protect them from destruction as a result of the Roman attack on the city.

There has been speculation that Jesus may have had connections with one of the communities that produced these documents, specifically the Essenes. Many similarities exist between the practices of the Essenes and those of the early Christians. Both groups were critical of mainstream Judaism and both engaged in baptism as an initiation ceremony. Ritual meals were also important for both and they each had a messianic focus, looking forward to the coming of an apocalyptic figure.

While the extent to which both

groupings could have identified with each other, and any involvement of Jesus himself, are the subjects of intense and ongoing debate, scholars believe that both communities reflect the religious concerns within first century CE Judaism, and responded in some similar ways, although they will also have differed considerably in their theology and world-view.

Since the Qumran community would probably have been in existence prior to the birth of Christ, could it have had some influence on the development of Christianity? The evidence that has come to light is ambiguous.

Some scholars see the Qumran community as espousing a world-view entirely at odds with that of Christianity, while others argue for a strong identification between Jesus and a key figure who emerges from the Qumran texts of the Essenes, the Teacher of Righteousness. The distinguished biblical scholar F. F. Bruce cautiously advances the view that John the Baptist may have been influenced by Qumran, but he discerns radical differences between the character of Jesus' ministry and the message of Qumran, while acknowledging certain similar resonances and themes.

The Apocrypha

The Apocrypha,[3] also known as the Deuterocanonical books, are a set of writings composed between the last writings of the Hebrew Bible and the New Testament period. Hence, they are often referred to as 'intertestamental'. The term *apocrypha* means 'hidden' or 'secret'. Bibles published in Protestant traditions place the apocryphal books into a separate section between the Old and New Testaments. The Protestant view, shared by Judaism, is that these books are not canonical. This means they do not have the same authority as the other scriptures of the Old and New Testaments. However, Roman Catholics and Christians from the Orthodox traditions regard some of the books as having canonical authority. Roman Catholic Bibles include amongst the Old Testament scriptures the seven books of Tobit, Judith, Wisdom, Sirach, 1 and 2 Maccabees, and Baruch and additional text in the books of Daniel and Esther.

Opinions on the status of the Apocrypha

There were wide differences of opinion in the early church about the authority of the apocryphal books, which indicates their importance. However, the biblical scholar Jerome, living in the late fourth century CE, argued for the separation of the books from the canon of the Hebrew Bible owing to what he believed to be their secondary status, and he was the first scholar to describe them as 'Apocrypha'. In the fifth century CE, Augustine championed their inclusion in the wider canon of scripture, but their doctrinal influence remained minimal.

The Protestant reformers, keen to establish what was true scripture and what was not, disapproved of many of the teachings and examples contained within the Apocrypha and felt that they were not in keeping with true biblical doctrine. Martin Luther had a particular difficulty with 2 Maccabees 12:45–46, which advocated prayer for the dead. He included the Apocrypha in his 1534 translation of the Bible into German, but separated the books from the rest of the canon, a tradition subsequently followed by publishers of many Protestant Bibles. The Roman Catholic Council of Trent, responding to the Reformation as a whole in 1546, incorporated the seven aforementioned books into the canon of scripture, and they are used in Roman Catholic worship along with the rest of the canon.

The authority of the Bible

Christians differ in their view as to how much authority the historical writings of the Bible should exercise. Evangelical Christians tend to regard it as having central authority, believing that every part of it has been inspired by God. Many regard it as being incapable of containing error. Other Christians accept it as authoritative, but subject to interpretation in various contexts. They believe that its teaching is not static, or bound to any one theological viewpoint, but that as human knowledge increases and as society changes, so the Bible can be understood in other ways over time. Others regard it simply as a historical record of God's dealing with his people and as a valuable guide, but no more authoritative than that. All Christians use the same sacred writings, but Roman Catholics accept an extra category of books, known as the Apocrypha, and Roman Catholic Bibles contain these books as well.

Opposite page: The caves of Qumran, where the Dead Sea Scrolls were found in 1947. Qumran was the centre of the Essenes – a breakaway sect from Judaism – who chose to dwell at this site towards the end of the second century BCE.

THE COMPACT GUIDE TO WORLD RELIGIONS

Core Beliefs

Belief and practice tends to vary widely amongst the various main branches of the Christian church. There are, however, certain areas of belief that are largely common to all the major branches of Christianity.

Jesus and God

Christians believe in one God, who was fully revealed in Jesus of Nazareth. This one God is also the creator of all that exists. Human beings are made in his image. Humans sinned against God and this caused separation. Therefore, Jesus, the Son of God, was sent to reconcile humankind and God through his death on the cross, which was a sacrifice for the sin of humanity. The raising of Jesus from the dead, the resurrection, showed that Jesus had defeated the power of death and Jesus could ascend back to heaven. Christians who believe in him and give their lives to him are assured of salvation, of living with him in heaven for all eternity.

Initiation and ritual

Christians generally undergo initiation into the church and are *baptized*. How this is done varies from one denomination to another, but will involve either sprinkling with water or total immersion in water. Adults who wish to be initiated are often fully immersed. Not all churches practise infant baptism, and those that do often have a further ceremony of commitment which is undergone when children reach an age where they can make commitments for themselves. This is called *confirmation* and requires a reiteration of the vows made on the child's behalf at baptism, together with further promises to live the Christian life.

As part of weekly worship, and often daily worship, Christians will enact the breaking of bread and the drinking of wine which Jesus performed on the night before he was crucified.

A Macedonian Orthodox priest baptizes a young man in the river Matka, 15 km (9.3 miles) outside the capital, Skopje. Macedonian Orthodox are traditionally baptized in the Matka river, near an area where the oldest monasteries in Macedonia are situated.

This is known as *Holy Communion* or *The Lord's Supper*. Roman Catholics refer to it as the *Eucharist*, which means 'thanksgiving'.

The Trinity

Christians believe in one God who consists of three distinct 'persons'. Each member of the Trinity, whether the Father, Jesus the Son, or the Holy Spirit, is equally divine and has equal status. They always work together, although each member of the Trinity may have a distinct function. The Holy Spirit is the agent of God in the world and God is believed to work in the world through the Holy Spirit. So, when Mary was told that she was to conceive Jesus, this conception was by the power of the Holy Spirit (Luke 1:30–33).

For all Christians, Jesus is of ultimate significance. How Christians view Jesus and what they believe about him may vary widely. In the fourth century CE, Christian theologians at Nicea formulated what is known as the *Nicene Creed*, a series of statements of belief about Jesus, God, the Holy Spirit and the church. These form the common basis of belief, although interpretations of the statements do differ.

Worship and Festivals

To some extent, all of the churches and movements will share beliefs and practices such as baptism and the Lord's Supper, but will express these in different ways (see **Branches**, p. 21). Hymn-singing has always been a feature of Christian worship

and the New Testament records that this was something the early Christians did when they met, along with the Communion service or 'breaking of bread'.

The trinity is depicted in this painting by G. H. Mester, 1471.

Christmas

A popular and important Christian festival is Christmas, which recalls the birth of Jesus and is celebrated on 25 December. It is preceded by a period of preparation lasting about four weeks and known as Advent. During this season of preparation, people sing hymns known as carols. Christmas Day is marked by special church services and by the giving of gifts.

Epiphany

Epiphany, on 6 January, celebrates an event in Matthew's Gospel when wise men from the East travel to see the young Jesus. This is seen as demonstrating that Jesus was not only important to Jews in his local community, but to distant non-Jews too.

Lent

Lent lasts for forty days and recalls the journey of Jesus into the wilderness, where he was tempted by the devil.

During this period of time, Christians often deny themselves some of the usual pleasures of life and it is used by many as a time of spiritual preparation for what is the most important feast of the Christian year, Easter.

Easter

This festival takes place after Lent and at the end of a special week known as Holy Week. This solemn period calls to mind the death of Jesus on the cross. The event is particularly marked on Good Friday. Following the solemnity of Lent and Holy Week, Easter Sunday is a day of celebration, when lively church services are held, churches are decorated in flowers and colour and children are given chocolate Easter eggs to eat.

A worshipper prays during a healing and deliverance convention led by Father Rufus Pereira, a Roman Catholic priest and exorcist appointed by Pope John Paul II, in Hyderabad, 2009. The six-day convention stresses repentance during the season of Lent, which culminates in Easter.

Family and Society

Early Christianity placed importance on the family unit, but power and influence often became concentrated in monastic institutions and the clerical classes where celibacy was encouraged. Another feature of early Christianity was the movement of ascetics into desert places, a lifestyle not conducive to family life. As a result, Christianity in the early centuries and in the Middle Ages often faced a paradox when it came to the family. It strongly supported traditional marriage and the raising of children within marriage, but lay people, both married and single, usually found themselves outside the power structures which became the preserve of a largely celibate clergy.

Christianity in modern times has continued to place great store on the family as a key building block of society, holding out marriage between one man and one woman as the ideal. Thus, many churches find it difficult to integrate divorced people or those who have had civil ceremonies. However, in the twentieth and early twenty-first centuries the percentage of marriages taking place in churches in the West has fallen sharply and the influence of traditional church teaching on daily life is clearly declining.

If the trend is to change, many Christians believe the church should be less focused on sexual morality and appreciate that morality extends to the social and economic spheres. They compare the history of the early church and the original vision of Jesus with more recent periods in history when the church has allied itself with the powerful and not championed the needs of the powerless and the displaced. In South America, in particular, Christians have formulated a theological approach that places social justice and freedom from physical poverty at the centre of the Christian search for salvation, alongside spiritual liberation.

Salt and light

Christians believe it is important to engage with society and culture. Over the past two centuries in particular Christians have become increasingly involved in public bodies, in politics and in the community. It is a core area of Christian teaching that Christians are to influence the societies in which they live, based on the stipulation of Jesus that they should be 'salt' and 'light' (Matthew 5:13–16).

This has led some to become involved in action to alleviate poverty, with the establishment of charities such as Tearfund and CAFOD (the Catholic Agency for Overseas Devlopment). Christians are often at the forefront of movements for peace, such as Quakers and Mennonites in the US and the Christian Campaign for Nuclear Disarmament (CCND) in Britain.

Contemporary Issues

Whereas Christianity in the Western world has suffered some decline, especially in Europe, the non-Western church has seen considerable growth in numbers, particularly in Africa, Asia, and Latin America. More contemporary forms of Christian practice, often based

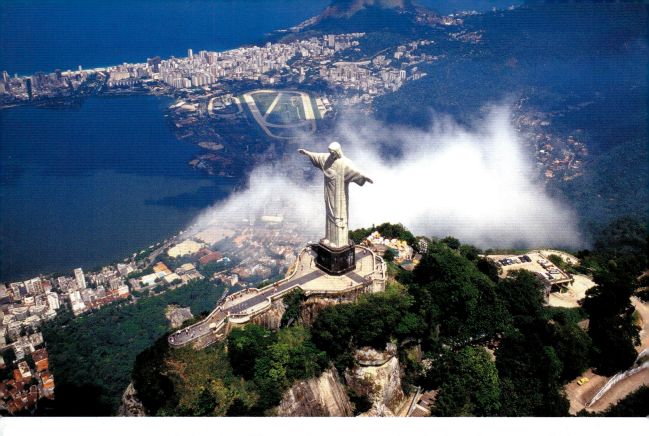

Aerial view of the Corcovado Christ Statue, Rio de Janeiro, Brazil.

on charismatic and Pentecostal-type worship and church structures, have made significant inroads in non-Western contexts. Church adherence in North America is still high in comparison to the rest of the Western world, but the projections for growth here are conservative in comparison to the projections for Latin America, Africa and Asia. Growth is especially apparent in church bodies and denominations that describe themselves as evangelical.

Moral conflicts and declining influence

Contemporary Christianity faces challenges from secular society and from competing faith systems. It also faces a great deal of internal conflict. The issue of homosexuals in church ministry is one which is causing very clear divisions in both Western and non-Western situations. Many of the more conservative church bodies in Africa are strongly opposed to homosexuality and the prospect of allowing the ordination of homosexuals and same-sex marriage in churches has led many to consider schism.

The ordination of women to church ministry is also a contentious issue in many places. Although several mainstream Protestant denominations have had female ministers for a number of years, the Roman Catholic Church remains firmly opposed to the ordination of women and in the main opposes married clergy.

Since the time of the early church fathers, abortion has been a matter of moral debate. In the US in particular it has become a very divisive issue.

Christian churches have had to face the stark reality that they are now in the religious marketplace along with many other faiths. In past times, especially in Europe and North America, Christianity enjoyed a privileged place in society and was granted a special status. Now, it finds itself 'amongst the faiths' and faces challenges not only from the major world religions, but from a growth in interest in the supernatural and the spiritual, expressed through the movement known as the New Age, an umbrella term that encompasses a number of new and old spiritualities.

Reading guide to Christianity

Green, Michael, ed., *The Truth of God Incarnate*, Hodder and Stoughton, London, 1977.

Hauerwas, Stanley & Wells, Samuel, ed., *The Blackwell Companion to Christian Ethics*, Blackwell Publishing, Oxford, 2004.

Hick, John, ed., *The Myth of God Incarnate*, SCM Press, London, 1977.

Hill, Jonathan, *The History of Christianity*, Lion, Oxford, 2007.

Hoose, Bernard, ed., *Christian Ethics*: *An Introduction*, Cassell, London, 1988.

Hunter, James Davison, *Evangelicalism*: *The Coming Generation,* University of Chicago Press, Chicago and London, 1987.

Jones, Gareth, *Christian Theology*: *A Brief Introduction*, Polity Press, Cambridge, 1999.

Lawrence, Paul, *The Lion Atlas of Bible History*, Lion, Oxford, 2006.

McGrath, Alister, ed., *The Blackwell Encyclopedia of Modern Christian Thought*, Blackwell Publishing, Oxford, 1997 edn.

McGrath, Alister, *Christian Theology*: *An Introduction*, Blackwell, Oxford, 1999 edn.

McKenzie, Peter, *The Christians*: *Their Practices and Beliefs*, SPCK, London, 1988.

Schmitals, Walter, *The Theology of the First Christians*, Westminster John Knox Press, Louisville, Kentucky, 1997.

Stott, John, *Issues Facing Christians Today*, Zondervan, Grand Rapids, Michigan, 2006, fourth edn.

Strange, Roderick, *The Catholic Faith*, Oxford University Press, Oxford, 1996 edn.

Woodhead, Linda, *An Introduction to Christianity*, Cambridge University Press, 2004.

Wright, N. T., *The Challenge of Jesus*, SPCK, London, 2000.

Judaism

History and Development

Judaism has long been practised throughout the world. For most of its history it has existed in the form of a strong and vibrant diaspora. In addition to the larger communities in Israel and North America, approximately half a million Jews live in South America and others live in various areas of the Middle East, Asia, Australia, and Africa.

Size Approximately 14 million adherents (6 million in North America; 4.5 million in Israel and 3 million in Europe).

Founder Devout Jews believe that God established a covenant with the patriarch Abraham and that this event signalled the beginning of the Jewish faith.

Location Originating in the area of the Middle East now known as Israel and the surrounding region in the third millennium BCE approximately.

It would be incorrect to think of Judaism as purely a religious phenomenon. Devout Jews view the practice of their faith as springing from their Jewish identity. This does not make the Jews a separate race, since Jews are to be found in all races and some non-Jews convert to Judaism (although to be regarded as a Jew by the most Orthodox one needs to have a Jewish mother). It does mean that, to a Jew, religious belief is only one aspect of his or her Judaism.

Formative influences in historical context

Throughout its history, Judaism has both influenced and been influenced by the myriad cultures around it. The history of Judaism begins with the story of Abraham, who lived in the third millennium BCE. Having received a revelation and directions from God, Abraham moved with his family to the land that surrounded the Sea of Galilee and the Dead Sea. They were told that this was the land of promise. The idea of covenant is crucial here since it explains the relationship Jews believe Abraham, their father in faith, had with God. They are thus known as 'the people of the covenant'. This covenant was continued through Abraham's descendants. His son Isaac in turn had a son Jacob, who also came to be known as 'Israel', the name of the modern Jewish state. One of Jacob's sons, Joseph, achieved high office in Egypt. Following

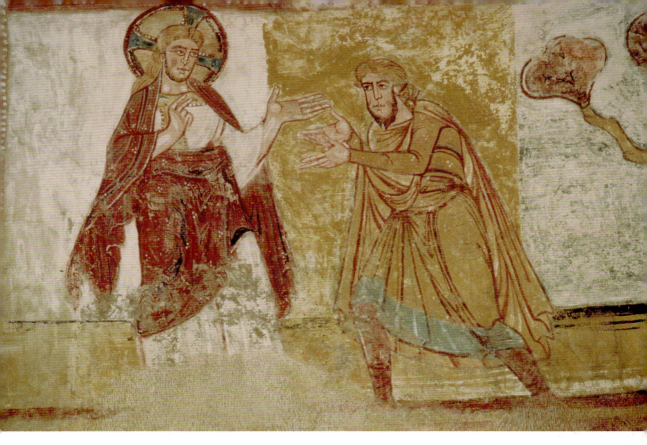

his death, the Israelites were enslaved by the Egyptians until they were freed from their captivity in dramatic fashion by God, through his agent, Moses. The Passover meal celebrates the night of Passover when Moses led the Israelites out of Egypt, in about 1300 BCE.

It was during this period that the Israelites were also given the Ten Commandments. Settling in a land that they made their own, the Jewish people established a monarchy and all the functions of state and religion, but continued to live in an unstable region in unstable times. Following the death of King Solomon, the kingdom split into two, the northern kingdom being styled as Israel and the southern as Judah. The northern kingdom was attacked by the Assyrians, the southern kingdom by the Babylonians.

Late 11th-century wall painting, in which God gives Abraham his commands. The painting was found in the nave in the monastery church at Saint-Savin, Department of Vienne, France.

The Babylonian captivity

In the sixth century BCE, at the height of Persian power, Jerusalem was destroyed by Nebuchadnezzar II and the people taken into captivity in Babylon. Some years later, Babylon was itself taken by Cyrus II of Persia and the Jews were allowed to return to their land. The Jews who returned re-established the Temple and its worship. The Temple, built in the tenth century

BCE, had been the most important centre of Jewish worship. Attempts were made by the Temple priests to enforce separation of Jew from non-Jew and to insist on ritual purity for Jews. The Jewish faith was beginning to establish its foundations for the future and organize itself as a system of belief and practice. In other Jewish communities – spread throughout Egypt, Babylon and other lands – Jews continued to observe their faith through establishing places of worship known as synagogues. The reign of Alexander the Great, which followed after 333 BCE, led to a period of prosperity in the region and established the Greek language and Greek culture. In this period the Jews spread widely, even establishing themselves as far as northern Spain.

The impact of Roman rule

Later, the Romans established their empire in the Jewish land in 63 BCE and it was during Roman rule that the desire for a

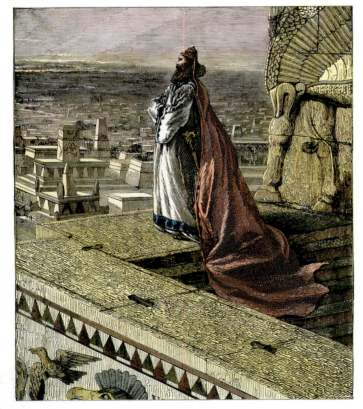

king after the line of King David became a strong aspiration amongst the Jews, leading to the emergence of numerous revolutionary movements. This led to a revolt in 66 CE by the Jews against Roman rule. The Romans sacked Jerusalem and destroyed the Temple in 70 CE. There was now no central seat of authority for Judaism. The establishment of Christianity and the presence of Jewish Christianity had already been posing a significant challenge to Jewish identity and authority. After the fall of Jerusalem, the Jews dispersed throughout the known world. The history of Jewish development in the lands to which it dispersed is a chequered one. Jews constantly found themselves in a minority position in other lands. Sometimes

they experienced periods of peace and prosperity, but at other times they were at the mercy of fluctuating political climates and often found themselves the objects of persecution. The rise of Christianity to become the state religion of the Roman empire marginalized Judaism further and put limits on its freedom.

Anti-Semitism

With the rise of Islam, Jews often found themselves in positions of influence in Islamic societies, but they were still subject to the vagaries of the changing political situation. In the Middle Ages Jews in Europe suffered a very high degree of anti-Semitism. They were expelled from Spain in 1492. At various periods in modern history they have been either hated and feared or treated with great tolerance and respect for their intellectual achievements, depending on the conditions of the time. The hatred of Jews culminated with the Holocaust (known also as the *Shoah*) when 6 million Jews were killed in Adolf Hitler's 'final solution' during the period of the Second World War, 1939–45. Afterwards there was a general will among Jews worldwide to establish a land of their own, under their own control, which they could live in and defend or support financially from abroad as a refuge in time of need.

Founder and Significant Figures

The Jewish or Hebrew scriptures give a detailed account of many influential figures involved with the development of Judaism. Throughout Jewish history, numerous

The Roman Titus Arch, dating from the 1st century BCE. The stone carving shows the seven-branched candlestick and other treasures being carried away by the victorious Romans.

kings, prophets, priests, patriarchs and ordinary individuals have been credited with extraordinary contributions to the faith.

Abraham

Abraham is regarded as the father of the Jewish people. Abraham lived in Ur of the Chaldees, situated around the mouth of the Rivers Tigris and Euphrates, in modern-day Iraq. He set out on a journey to find the land promised to him by God, the land of Canaan. The book of Genesis, which records the story, tells that God established an agreement, or covenant, with Abraham. Abraham was to worship only one god and in turn this God would bless him and give to him the land of Canaan. It is on the basis of this promise to Abraham that Jews have laid claim to the land now called Israel.

Moses and the exodus from Egypt

One of the most important people in Hebrew scripture and in the development of Jewish identity is Moses, who was born to a Hebrew slave in Egypt. As a baby, he was hidden away for safety and placed in a basket on the River Nile. Found by the pharaoh's daughter, he was raised as an Egyptian, but later embraced his Jewish identity. Turning his back on his Egyptian life, he intervened on behalf of a Hebrew slave who was being ill-treated by an Egyptian taskmaster. He killed the taskmaster and went on the run. Moses had a profound experience of God and believed himself called to be the instrument that would persuade Pharaoh to set the Hebrew people free.

The pharaoh whom Moses had defied in killing the Egyptian was no longer in power, so Moses challenged the new ruler to free the Hebrew slaves. When this pharaoh refused, Moses called down a series of calamities, or plagues, on the Egyptians until he relented. In an event still marked each year by Jews, Moses led the people out of Egypt as the angel of death descended on the male first-born of every household in Egypt. The Hebrews were protected by the blood of a lamb smeared on the lintels of their doors, which caused the angel to 'pass over' their homes, sparing them. Once a year, Jews celebrate Passover with a traditional meal.

Moses led the people through the desert wilderness and shaped them as a nation. Devout Jews believe that while in the desert, Moses received from God the Ten Commandments, which form the basis of Jewish ethical teaching, and the Torah, or the written Jewish teaching texts.

Moses is shown with the tablets of the Law (anon.), c.1600–25.

Branches of Judaism

Over the centuries many branches and sects have grown up within Judaism. Some of the divisions are cultural, others are religious. The main groups that have a European origin are the *Ashkenazim* and the *Sephardim*. The *Ashkenazim* have their European origins in central and eastern Europe and the Yiddish language developed here. The *Sephardic* Jews have a Spanish and Portuguese origin and these Jews developed their own *Ladino* language. Both groupings are important in world Judaism today and those who have settled in

the land of Israel bring with them their own cultural styles. Each has its own chief rabbi.

Orthodox Judaism

Orthodox Jews tend to regard only 'observant Jews' as true Jews. They believe that the absolute divine origin of both the written and oral Torah gives it an unchanging authority. The laws of the Torah affect every area of life in minute detail and 'observant Jews' are very particular about keeping them. Strict adherence to rigid dietary laws and rules governing ritual purity is expected. In modern times, many Orthodox Jews have expressed the necessity of some accommodation with the secular world and pursue careers and study within

Left: In this 1880 woodcut, the expulsion of the Jews from Spain in 1492 is depicted. The Grand Inquisitor, Thomas de Torquemada, obtains their expulsion on 31 March 1492.

contemporary culture, but taking care to ensure that the strict laws governing Orthodoxy are obeyed. Those Orthodox Jews who advocate greater contact with the world system are also known as Neo-Orthodox.

Hasidic Jews

The *Hasidim* or Hasidic Jews regard themselves as being Ultra-Orthodox in their approach to the world. They adhere to a strict code of dress, which basically consists of a wide-brimmed black hat, a black coat and long, curled hair locks,

or ringlets, hanging down by each ear. The *Hasidim* place great emphasis on the mystical side of the Jewish faith and it is within Hasidism that we find teaching on the *Kabbalah*, which encourages a mystical interpretation of scripture, with great attention given to symbolism and allegorical and secret meaning.

Orthodox Lelov Jews at the Synagogue in Hebron, part of the religious site known to both Jewish and Muslim worshippers as the Tomb of the Patriarchs.

Reform Judaism

Reform Judaism emerged out of a desire to harmonize Judaism with progressive movements within Western society in particular. Following on from Enlightenment principles, the Reform movement moved away from strict interpretation of the Torah and left it up to the individual believer to develop his or her own interpretation and apply it in life according to individual circumstances. Reform Judaism increasingly viewed the Torah as not having a purely divine origin. It was considered to be of human authorship, under divine guidance, but with inevitable human interpretation and bias. As a result it was open to a wide range of approaches. Reform Jews try to accommodate modern scientific discoveries into their understanding of the world and how the cosmos was created. They do not adhere to strict dietary laws or ritual practices, regarding these as reflecting the human and cultural concerns of the time in which they were written, and so not binding on contemporary Judaism. Reform Judaism accepts women rabbis. In Reform Jewish congregations, men and women are not segregated but sit together and women, as well as being rabbis, are also able to fulfil all of the functions traditionally performed by men.

Conservative Jews

Conservative Judaism arose as a reaction against Reform Judaism. Many Jews were unhappy with what they regarded as the extremes to which Reform Judaism had gone. Conservative Judaism tries to steer a more middle path. It began in the US and tries to combine the best of both Orthodox and Reform Judaism, believing that progress is necessary, but that important matters of tradition should not be cast lightly aside. Conservative Judaism has also sought to give more influence to women. It encourages involvement in national life but also stresses the need for Jews to maintain a distinctive character in society.

Sacred Writings

The most important of the Jewish scriptures is the Torah, which consists of the first five books of what is known as the Pentateuch, also known as the Five Books of Moses – that is, Genesis, Exodus, Leviticus, Numbers and Deuteronomy. The collective name for the Jewish scriptures is *Tenakh* (from the names of the three parts). The *Tenakh* is made up of the Torah, the *Nevi'im* and the *Ketubim*.

The Torah

The term *torah* refers to 'instruction' or 'teaching', but it is usually translated as 'Law'. It provides instruction as to how people should live their lives. It expresses how God works in creation and in history. It is believed that God is speaking directly to the Jewish people through the Torah. Words from the Torah – particularly the words in Deuteronomy known as the *Shema*, which instruct the Jewish people, 'Hear O Israel, the Lord our God is one. And you shall love the Lord thy God with all thy heart and with all thy soul and with all thy might' (Deuteronomy 6:4–6) – are written down and placed in small metal containers known as *mezuzahs* on the lintels of the outside doors of Jewish homes.

The Torah is interpreted differently in the various branches of Judaism. This job is given to the rabbis, who are the Jewish teachers. It is their responsibility to interpret the ways in which Jewish law should be applied.

The Torah in Jewish worship

The Torah is an important feature and focus of Jewish collective worship. This takes place in the synagogue. In Orthodox Judaism only men can read from the Torah. The Torah is kept, in the form of a scroll, in a cupboard known as the ark, which faces Jerusalem. During worship, it is removed from the ark and its ornate and embroidered protective cloth covering is taken off. It is then paraded around the synagogue in a short procession.

A rabbi reads the Torah before a Hasidic congregation at the Synagogue of the Premishlan in Bnei Brak, Israel.

The men in the congregation, wearing prayer shawls known as *tallit* shawls, will touch the scrolls with the tassels, known as *tzitzit*, attached to the shawls. After this the Torah is placed on a raised reading desk. From there it is read to the congregation. Out of reverence the reader will not touch the scroll text while reading, but will follow the words with a special pointer called a *yad*, usually made of silver. The scroll will usually be topped with a crown, signifying its importance. When a Jewish boy reaches the age of thirteen, he is made a 'son of the commandment' or Bar Mitzvah and is trained to read a part of the scroll. Within Reform Judaism, girls go through a Bat Mitzvah.

The Tenakh
The Nevi'im
This refers to the books of the Prophets. These are books found in the Hebrew Bible that contain the sayings and teachings of people who, it is believed, are speaking on behalf of God himself. It was the job of the prophets to remind the Jews of the law of God and to ensure that the people returned to faith when they had wandered from it. The *Nevi'im* are divided into sections which deal with categories of the prophets and prophetic texts.

The Ketubim
Also called 'Collected Writings', the *Ketubim* contain eleven books – Psalms, Proverbs, Job, Song of Songs, Ruth, Lamentations, Ecclesiastes, Esther, Daniel, Ezra, and Nehemiah. The book of Psalms is of particular importance in worship and it is viewed as man speaking to God and expressing both reverence and prayer.

When the first letters of Torah, *Nevi'im* and *Ketubim* are taken together, they spell out T,N,K, from which comes the word *Tenakh*.

The Mishnah
The *Mishnah* is a kind of oral Torah. As rabbis through the ages discussed their opposing interpretations of the Torah, these were handed down by oral transmission. Eventually they were recorded and are known as *Mishnah*. The rulings are almost like an extra layer of laws that protect the central laws from being transgressed. The *Mishnah* deals with different aspects of daily life, such as agriculture, festivals, marriage and divorce, civil and criminal law, Temple sacrifice and laws which govern dietary issues, laws and ritual purification.

The *Mishnah* itself became the subject of much interpretation and re-interpretation. A text called the *Gemara* recorded the discussions of influential rabbis about the text of the *Mishnah*. The integration of the *Mishnah* with the *Gemara* is known as the *Talmud*. Not surprisingly, the *Talmud* is an extremely long document of something like four million words.

Midrash is a continual commentary on all of the texts of Judaism.

Core Beliefs

To the Jews, God, who has revealed himself, is at the very centre of their belief system. The idea of covenant is an important concept within Judaism. It defines the Jew's relationship with God, which is a mutual one.

The concept of God

Within Judaism, God is traditionally viewed as being transcendent, in that he is entirely distinct from the created order. At the same time he is believed to be intimately involved with world history and with the history of the Jewish people in particular. Over the centuries, Judaism has become a very diverse faith with many branches, and beliefs tend to differ according to which branch of Judaism is being explored. Beliefs that traverse the whole of the spectrum are those which are centred on the nature and function of God. Jews believe that their scriptures chronicle the history of God's relationship with the world and with the Jews. These scriptures also set out the basis for human beings' relationship with each other. Maimonides, the name by which Rabbi Moshe Ben Maimon (1135–1204) is also known, set out thirteen principles of faith which defined the nature and function of God within the Jewish faith. Maimonides stressed the 'oneness' of God and the fact that he was creator of the universe. God is not corporeal and has no beginning or end. Prayer should be directed to him alone and to no other. Maimonides laid particular emphasis on the truth of Jewish revelation, particularly the words of the prophets, the teaching of Moses and of course the Torah.

The Chabad members pray at the synagogue in Pinczow, Poland.

The *Kabbalah*

The Jewish *kabbalah*[1] can best be described as an esoteric path. It is concerned with a series of teachings about the inner life and explores the inner nature of God. The word *kabbalah* means 'tradition'. Those who practise it understand it as a corpus of secret and sacred doctrines that reveal the inner, hidden meaning of the Torah.

This mystical system has achieved fresh attention from the latter part of the twentieth century and into the twenty-first. The principal text of kabbalism is the *Zohar*, a medieval work, begun in the thirteenth century but finished in the sixteenth, which draws on earlier Gnostic philosophical ideas. The *Zohar* was written to be a commentary on the Pentateuch and the books which comprise the five scrolls (namely Esther, Ruth, Song of Songs, Ecclesiastes or Qoheleth, and Lamentations).

Kabbalism teaches that there are two aspects to the revelation of God. One is exoteric and reveals what God does and what God desires; the other is esoteric and explores who God is in himself.

- The scriptures, according to *kabbalah*, have both literal meaning and deeper, more symbolic resonances. Kabbalism claims to explain the hidden meanings.
- God in himself is *Ein Sof*, that is, he is boundless and limitless. He is infinity.
- *Ein Sof* is manifested through ten emanations which are known as the *Sefirot*.
- Through the *Sefirot* humankind is able to engage with God.

There are various approaches to the *kabbalah* within Judaism, ranging from outright acceptance to deep suspicion on the grounds that it is a form of imported paganism.

Reform Judaism regards kabbalism as akin to superstition, but is aware that it contains useful insights into the Torah and Jewish history. Hasidic Judaism has appropriated many ideas and teachings from kabbalist sources. Many Orthodox Jews are cautious about kabbalist teaching, believing that kabbalist texts and doctrines should not be studied by novices but rather by those who are skilled enough and strong enough to discern what is true from what is false.

God knows, Maimonides wrote, the heart and the deeds of all humankind. He rewards those who follow his commandments and punishes those who do not. Maimonides mentions the concept of the all-important messiah, who is expected and who will come.

The covenant

In Jewish belief, God controls the universe and directs it in its purpose. The Jews believe themselves to be the chosen people of God, chosen to manifest God's purpose and God's desires to the whole of the human race. The covenant made between God and Noah is seen as the first evidence of this mutual agreement between God and humankind (Genesis 9:8–17). Then, the Abrahamic covenant of Genesis 15 and 17 includes the commitment to give to the Jewish people the Promised Land. The covenant is cemented again in the time of Moses and it forms a continual backdrop against which the history of the people of Israel unfolds. An important part of the Mosaic covenant is the giving of the Ten Commandments to Moses at Mount Sinai.

Worship and Festivals

Jewish worship is lively and vibrant, with special dates and events celebrated or remembered throughout the year both in the home and at the synagogue.

Sabbath

The weekly Sabbath, which lasts from sunset on Friday to sunset on Saturday, is regarded as a day of rest, the Hebrew word

Shabbat meaning 'rest'. It is a day when devout Jews think about God and the things of God. It has its roots in the Genesis account of creation, when God himself rested from work, but it is also a feature of the covenant in Exodus 31:16, 17 where we are told, 'Therefore the people of Israel shall keep the Sabbath throughout their generations, as a perpetual covenant.'

Jews attend synagogue services on the Sabbath. Orthodox Jews are strict about Sabbath worship and refuse to do any kind of work at all on that day. Conservative Jews also take the Sabbath very seriously. There are strict rules governing what can and cannot be done. Very religious Jews will not engage in long journeys on the Sabbath, answer the telephone or cook food.

The Sabbath is celebrated with a traditional meal and Sabbath candles are lit. Blessings are spoken before, over, and after food. The meal includes bread and wine and other symbolic foods. Special *hallah* bread is used. It reminds Jews of the heavenly food or *manna* provided by God for the people of Israel when they wandered in the wilderness. The bread and other food may be wrapped in special cloths. The best crockery and table ornamentation is used.

A woman prays before Shabbat candles.

Left: A 1604 Kabbalistic scroll with illuminations, containing descriptions of the names of God, the Sefirot, the 32 paths, the mystery of the letters and vowels, and various items from the Temple.

Praying

Jews who are committed to their faith try to pray three times a day. Men will cover their heads with a *yarmulke* or *kippah*, a kind of skull-cap. A prayer shawl or *tallit* will cover the shoulders. This has its origins in Exodus 15:37–40, where Moses is told to instruct the people to wear a shawl with tassels at the corners, each tassel having a cord of blue 'to look upon and remember all the commandments of the Lord'. In addition *tefillin* or phylacteries are worn: small boxes containing words of scripture, strapped to either the forehead or left arm. They fulfil the command for Jews to keep the Law in front of them and close at all times.

Traditionally, Judaism has been a religion where men take the lead in worship. Women were not encouraged to read and study the Torah or could be forbidden to do so, depending on the particular culture and strand of Judaism. In modern times women are encouraged to study it, except in the most orthodox streams of the faith, and even in some of these the situation is changing. Reform and Conservative Judaism both allow women to become rabbis. However, in the most orthodox and ultra-orthodox branches of Judaism, women are not permitted to sit with men in the synagogue and are not able to count as part of the quorum or *minyan*, the group of ten Jewish males who must be present for communal worship to take place. In such traditions, women are encouraged to pray, but this prayer is of a private nature.

Even within Orthodox Judaism, however, women are exploring feminist approaches to the faith and are trying to promote a greater role for themselves within the worshipping community. As a result, some Orthodox rabbis allow women to gather together in prayer groups, where many also study the Torah.

Synagogue

Regular weekly worship and worship on annual festivals takes place at the synagogue. Synagogues are generally organized in three main parts according to the layout of the Temple at Jerusalem. The scrolls which contain the Torah are kept in the ark. The organization of the synagogue reflects the most important features of Jewish belief. The Ten Commandments are featured somewhere around the ark, on either side or above. The *menorah*, a seven-branched candelabrum, is kept by the side of the ark. In front of the ark is placed a light, the *ner tamid* or 'perpetual light', which is kept continually burning to indicate the presence of God.

Passover

Once a year, during the Jewish month of *Nisan*, the Passover is remembered. This festival is also known as *Pesah*. It is a highly symbolic occasion, the symbolism representing the flight from Egypt. It calls to mind how the angel of death 'passed over' the homes of the Hebrew people, sparing them. The festival lasts eight days and the central point is the Passover meal or *Seder*.

The Hebrews did not have time to allow their bread to rise before they left Egypt, so

Other important festivals

Rosh Hashanah, the New Year festival in the Jewish month of *Tishri*, generally lasting two days	Sweet foods are eaten to symbolize blessing and goodness. *Rosh Hashanah* celebrates events in the lives of those important to the Jewish faith, such as the birthdays of Adam, Abraham, Isaac and Jacob, and the escape from captivity of Joseph and Moses. Jews make resolutions for the year ahead and ask forgiveness for the sins of the past year. The ram's horn or *shofar* is blown regularly in worship services throughout the festival.
Yom Kippur, a few days after *Rosh Hashanah*	The Day of Atonement, the most serious and the holiest day in the Jewish calendar, is particularly a time for asking for forgiveness for sin. People fast on this day and attend worship services at the synagogue and recommit themselves to God.
Hanukkah, an eight-day festival which begins during the month of *Kislev*	This 'festival of light' celebrates an event in 165 BCE when the Temple at Jerusalem was re-dedicated to God (following its defilement by the Greeks, who placed pagan idols in it and forced the Jews to worship them).
Sukkot, in the month of *Tishri*	This 'feast of tabernacles' calls to mind how the Jewish people lived in 'booths' when they journeyed through the wilderness and how God protected them.
Purim, celebrated in the month of *Asdar*	This festival reminds Jews of a very important event from the book of Esther, in which Esther – forced to marry the Persian king, Ahasuerus – frustrates the attempts of his advisors to murder the Jews. *Purim* is a time of great joy and the story of Esther is read in the synagogue.

they had to eat unleavened bread (Exodus 12:39). Thus today, during Passover, no leavened bread is allowed into the Jewish home. Anything containing yeast is considered impure. The *Seder* takes place on the first night of Passover and great care is undertaken to ensure that the family table is beautifully decorated. It is set with various foods, all of symbolic value, and the meal proceeds according to a strict order of service. Four cups of wine are drunk in a defined sequence and the story of the original Passover is told by the father of the house in response to questions from the youngest child. Songs of praise are sung. A roasted shank bone of lamb at the table represents the Passover lamb (a symbol which has taken on particular resonance within Christianity). Bitter herbs, also known as *maror*, are eaten to remind Jews of the bitterness of captivity. Almonds, apple and wine are mixed into a paste known as *charoseth*. This stands for the mortar used in building, a task which the Hebrews had to engage in while in slavery. Salt water is placed on the table to symbolize the tears shed by the Jews while they were enslaved.

Family and Society

Marriage

Marriage or *kiddushin* is generally conducted with another Jew. It is unusual, though no longer so rare, for a Jew to 'marry out', that is, marry a non-Jew or Gentile. The marriage between a man and a woman is considered to be reminiscent of

Circumcision

The act of circumcision[2] is a sign of the covenant which, Genesis teaches, was made between God and his people. In Hebrew the 'covenant of circumcision' is known as *berit milah* and has its origins in God's dealings with Abraham. Abraham, who has undergone circumcision himself, is told to circumcise his male descendants (Genesis 17:9–13). It is therefore a sign made in the very flesh.

In general Jewish boys are circumcised at eight days old. It involves cutting off the foreskin of the penis. Ideally the ceremony takes place in the presence of a quorum of ten adult males. A chair is set out for the prophet Elijah, who is asked to bear witness to the faithfulness of the people of Israel in observing the covenant. The man tasked with the ritual act is known as a *mohel*. During the ceremony frequent reference is made to Abraham, who himself circumcised his son Isaac.

In modern-day traditions of Judaism the birth of a daughter is celebrated in a liturgical rite known as the *simhat habat* or 'rejoicing over the birth of a daughter'.

the covenant between God and humankind. It is a sacred union. The service takes place usually in the synagogue. During the ceremony the bride and her husband stand under a canopy known as a *huppah*, which represents their new home together. Divorce is allowed within Judaism, but is discouraged.

Funerals

In Jewish funerals it is accepted as a fact of life that there is a limit to human existence. A Jew who is dying is encouraged, if able, to recite the *Shema.* If not, someone will do it on their behalf. At the funeral of a male Jew a prayer shawl or *tallit* – with one tassel cut off – will be placed on the coffin.

Funerals are usually simple and generally take place within twenty-four hours of death if this is possible. Relatives of the deceased will tear a piece of their clothing as a sign of mourning. This is called *keriah*. Following the funeral, a seven-day period of mourning is observed. During this time the mourners sit on low stools or on the floor and mirrors are kept covered.

Contemporary Issues

Over many centuries Jewish people have been subjected to anti-Semitism, hated and attacked and in the worst cases cruelly murdered, simply for not being someone else. To their murderers it has made scant difference whether they were devout Jews or non-believers. Naturally Jews continue to be on their guard against anti-Semitism, whether it raises its head in Europe, the old Soviet Republics or anywhere else in the world. It never seems to go away, although of course it is not the only issue that concerns Jews.

International relationships

Jews are generally considered to exercise a cultural, intellectual and religious influence far exceeding their numerical proportion within the world's population. In campaigns to protect or improve human rights Jews are always well represented. Only about 14 million Jews live in the world, yet their impact on world affairs is vast.

The foundation of Israel in 1948 has led to five wars between the Jews and their Arab neighbours about land and politics. The territorial claims of the Jewish people have not been universally accepted and the development or indeed existence of modern-day Israel is still a point of contention. The expansion of Jewish settlements on land that Palestinian Arabs consider their own continues to heighten tension within the region and with the Palestinian community. While the Hebrew scriptures, devout Jews believe, particularly the covenant with Abraham, provide the theological justification for their claims to the land of Israel, these also record ancient conflicts in which the Jewish people used this justification as an imprimatur to enlarge their borders and sphere of influence forcibly.

The relationship between Israel and its closest ally, the US, also provokes controversy. Jewish groups enjoy high degrees of influence in US politics and are often accused of unfairly influencing US foreign policy. In many nations there is concern about Israel's possession of nuclear weapons and its use of military power in ways viewed as 'disproportionate' and thus illegal.

Within Judaism itself there is also debate about Israel, with most branches of Judaism remaining constant in strong support, although many Jews disagree with certain policies of the Israeli state. For example, should religious laws be given more prominence or, on the contrary, should the state be more secular and better able to accommodate non-Jewish citizens?

The direction of modern Judaism

There are strong internal debates within Judaism about the direction of the religion in the modern world and to what extent Jews should accommodate twenty-first-century cultural values. The Reform branch of Judaism has tried to create a greater degree of interaction between the faith

Left: A circumcision ceremony takes place at Stamford Hill Orthodox Jewish Community, London, UK.

Below: Men pray at the Western Wall in Jerusalem, Israel. The Western Wall is the holiest site in Judaism and is situated below the Dome of the Rock, Islam's second holiest site.

Reading guide to Judaism

Corrigan, John et al, ed., *Jews, Christians, Muslims: A Comparative Introduction to Monotheistic Religions*, Prentice-Hall, Inc., New Jersey, 1998.

De Lange, Nicholas, *Judaism*, Oxford University Press, Oxford, 1987.

De Lange, Nicholas, *An Introduction to Judaism*, Cambridge University Press, Cambridge, UK, 2000.

De Lange, Nicholas & Freud-Kandel, Miri, ed., *Modern Judaism: An Oxford Guide*, Oxford University Press, Oxford, 2005.

Kaplan, Mordecai, M., *The Meaning of God in Modern Jewish Religion*, Wayne State University Press, Detroit, 1994 edn.

Kellner, Menachem, *Must a Jew Believe Anything?*, Vallentine Mitchell, London and Portland, Oregon, 1999.

Neusner, Jacob et al ed., *Judaism and Islam in Practice*, Routledge, London, 2000.

Neusner, Jacob & Avery-Peck, Alan J., ed., *The Blackwell Reader in Judaism*, Blackwell Publishing, Oxford, 2001.

Neusner, Jacob & Avery-Peck, Alan J., ed., *The Blackwell Companion to Judaism*, Blackwell Publishing, Oxford, 2004 edn.

Neusner, Jacob, *The Emergence of Judaism*, Westminster John Knox Press, Louisville, Kentucky and London, 2004.

Neusner, Jacob, *Judaism in Contemporary Context: Enduring Issues and Chronic Crises*, Vallentine Mitchell, London and Portland, Oregon, 2007.

Partridge, Christopher, ed., *The World's Religions*, Lion, Oxford, 2005, third edn.

Unterman, Alan, *The Jews: Their Religious Beliefs and Practices*, Sussex Academic Press, Brighton, 1996, second and fully revised edn.

and contemporary society, moving away from the emphasis on Jews as a persecuted people and stressing the positive contributions that Jewish values and beliefs can make to the world. Conservative Jews try to interpret their faith in the context of modern values but with roots in traditional practice. Orthodox Jews generally want to observe the absolute authority of the Torah, although the Orthodox groupings do this to different degrees. Ultra-Orthodox Jews advocate the complete separation of Judaism from modernity.

Increasingly, there are Jews who do not consider themselves religious Jews, but who cherish their distinctive customs and identity. Indeed the greatest threat to Judaism today is probably that of secularism. With Jewish populations relatively small, more Jews now marry outside of the faith and traditions handed on through generations of Jewish households are losing their importance.

Islam

History and Development

'Islam' is an Arabic word, the root of which implies that peace is to be had through submission to the will of God. A Muslim is a follower of Islam and is someone who promises to submit his or her life to Allah. This concept of submission is therefore central to the faith.

Islam shares its roots with two other monotheistic faiths, and with them it traces its roots back to the patriarch Abraham, a figure who is sacred in the memory of both Judaism and Christianity. Ishmael, the son whom Abraham conceived with Hagar, is an important figure in Islamic history and theology. It is believed that together with Abraham, Ishmael built the *Ka'ba* at Mecca, a large cube that became a centre of pilgrimage and devotion, particularly of worship of the one God. Thus, even before the time of Muhammad, Mecca was an important religious centre.

Receiving God's message

Islam begins with the person of Muhammad, who was born in Mecca around 570 CE when Mecca was a major centre of trade in Arabia. His father died before he was born, so his mother Aminah named him Muhammad, believing with her father-in-law, 'Abd al-Muttalib, that God had chosen this child for something great. Muhammad means 'the praised one'.

Only six years old when Aminah died, Muhammad was placed in his grandfather's care. On his grandfather's death he went to work as a shepherd for his uncle, Abu Talib, and in the course of this employment he got the opportunity to travel widely. In 610 CE Muhammad believed he was hearing messages directly from God and that it was important to spread these messages. He gathered many followers around him, but

Size With approximately 1.5 billion adherents worldwide, Islam ranks as second largest amongst the religions of the world.

Founder Muslims believe that the Prophet Muhammad received a revelation from God.

Location Originating in the area around modern-day Saudi Arabia in approximately 610–630 CE, the religion is now worldwide. Today the majority of Muslims live in Asia, the Middle East, and North Africa.

faced great opposition from the merchants of Mecca, whose trade he threatened by preaching against idol worship.

Laying the foundations

In 622 CE Muhammad fled with his followers to Medina, now an important centre of pilgrimage in present-day Saudi Arabia. It was here that he consolidated Islamic teaching and religious practice. Growing in religious significance, Muhammad also grew in political influence and enacted several alliances with Jewish tribes. Having grown in political power, he attacked Mecca around 630 CE. After the death of Muhammad in 632 CE the religious path that he followed had grown not just into an organized faith system, but also a political entity.

The leaders who followed Muhammad, known as caliphs, grew in power as they raided the lands of the peoples surrounding them. Powerful though the caliphs became, Muhammad was regarded as the last of the prophets.

The spread of Islam

The influence of Islam spread through Egypt, Syria, Iraq, Libya, and Iran. Muslims made further alliances with local leaders and with Christian and Jewish communities. Muslim expansion continued apace for over a century, encompassing North Africa, southern France, Spain, Constantinople, Persia and moving into central Asia. Later, India fell under Islamic power.

After 750 CE the centre of Islamic power shifted from Damascus to Baghdad. Gradually, through the influence of traders, through conquest and through conversion, Islam became the dominant faith in large parts of Africa and Asia. Islamic law, known as *Shari'a*, developed over this period. By 1500 Muslims had been overcome and driven out of the Iberian peninsula, but had established a firm hold on Constantinople (modern-day Istanbul).

Founder and Significant Figures

The towering figure in the history of Islam is without question Muhammad (c. 570–632 CE). Following the death of his grandfather he worked for his uncle, during which time he gained a reputation for honesty and integrity. His reputation was to grow immeasurably.

Muhammad's vision

In the late sixth century Mecca was a lawless place. Clans and tribes fought with each other regularly. Gambling, excessive drinking and the ill-treatment of women were widespread. Idolatry was rife. Many gods were worshipped. Muhammad stood out as a man with the highest moral standards. At the age of twenty-five he went to work for a rich businesswoman called Khadijah, who was about forty. They married in 595 CE.

During the month of *Ramadan* in 610 CE Muhammad was in prayer, as was often his habit. Alone in a cave on Mount Hira he was visited by an angel, whose name was Jibril or Gabriel. Muhammad was shown a vision of a roll of silk on which were written letters that seemed to be made of fire. He was instructed to read the letters, although he was illiterate. He read, 'Recite, in the name of your Lord! He Who created! He created man from a blood clot.' These words are now in the ninety-sixth chapter or *surah* of the Qur'an.

The reception of the Qur'an

When Muhammad told Khadijah about the vision, she supported him and wondered if he was a prophet of God. As the years progressed, Muhammad heard more words from God. They encouraged him to speak out more forcefully against the idol worship he saw around him. This angered the Meccan merchants who made a good living from selling idols, from the sale of alcohol and from the proceeds of gambling. Muhammad's appeal to the poor disquieted the merchants too.

After about ten years of modest success in Mecca, Muhammad moved with his followers to Medina, a city about 300 kilometres (190 miles) from Mecca. This move to Medina is known within Islam as the *hijrah* and was the occasion of the true emergence of Islam into a solid system.

Society in Medina was divided, there being many different tribes and groups in the city. Muhammad set about creating some measure of unity and organization between these groups and his own followers so that he could begin to spread the message. He still faced opposition from many quarters. Muhammad failed at Medina to establish the relationship he wanted with Jews and Christians and this resulted in many killings. When his power base was stronger, he attacked Mecca and defeated it. He then set about work on the *Ka'ba* and destroyed the idols that had been placed in it in defiance of its Abrahamic origins.

Pakistani men pray at Friday prayers in the Lal Masjid (Red Mosque) in Islamabad, Pakistan.

Many stories are told about Muhammad and the protection and favour that he enjoyed from God or Allah. Once, when a group of assassins set out to kill him, he and his followers hid in a cave. A spider spun a web across the mouth of the cave and a bird made its nest over the entrance. The assassins assumed the cave had lain unused and unoccupied for a long time and did not enter it.

Muhammad died at Medina in 632 CE. Muslims revere him because they believe that he is a prophet who spoke the words of Allah. Every day Muslims say, 'There is no God but Allah and Muhammad is the messenger of Allah.'

Disagreements over successors

After Muhammad's death his followers were devastated, but they realized they needed to keep on preaching his message. He was succeeded first by Abu Bakr, his close follower, and subsequently by three other caliphs who carried on his work. A major dispute arose over the legitimacy of the fourth member of his entourage to succeed him, his cousin and son-in-law, Ali. It is because of this argument that Islam split into two main groupings, the *Sunni* and the *Shi'a*.

Branches of Islam

In modern times Islam has grown into a global religion, the second largest in the world. Most Muslims live in the Middle East and in Asia. Countries such as Indonesia and Malaysia have very large Muslim populations. Sizeable Muslim populations are also to be found among the peoples of eastern Europe and in the Central Asian republics of the former Soviet Union. Western Europe is also home to large numbers of Muslims, with an estimated total of 9 million Muslims living in the Netherlands, Germany and France, and about 2 million in Great Britain. Islam is a rapidly growing religion within the US and estimates of the Muslim population there vary from 4 to 12 million.

Sunni and Shi'a

The vast majority of Muslims, perhaps as many as 85 per cent, belong to the *Sunni* branch. Among the minority the *Shi'a* form much the largest group. Both Shi'a and Sunni Muslims share faith in the same God and belief in the same Qur'an and in Muhammad. However, their interpretations of Islamic history and of how leadership should be constituted differ. The main argument between them is based on the question of who should have succeeded Muhammad. It then spread from being a purely religious issue to being a political one as well and it has been a major factor in the hostilities between predominantly Sunni Iraq and Shi'a Iran.

Sufism

Sufism, which highlights the interior life, is not a branch of Islam in the sense that the Sunni and Shi'a groupings are. It is strongly concerned with discerning the presence of God, both in the world and in the human self. It is contemplative and is focused on the love of God and on God's mercy. It does not see itself as distinct or

Sunni Muslims

The Sunni accept the authority of the four caliphs who followed Muhammad. In modern times they see no need for a caliph to regulate the whole of Islam; they leave the governance of the faith to national bodies in Islamic societies.

Shi'a Muslims

The Shi'a look much more to *imams* for their spiritual authority, and the notion of a messianic twelfth *imam* who has been guiding the Shi'a spiritual leaders and will return to earth at an appointed time has very strong influence.

The term 'Shi'a' means followers or group, and Shi'a Islam was formed as a result of a dispute involving the followers of the fourth caliph, Ali. Ali's followers believed he should have been created as the first caliph and successor to Muhammad. Both Ali and his son Husayn were martyred, and this created a strong focus on suffering, persecution and martyrdom within Shi'a Islam. The Shi'a have always felt they have been persecuted because of their interpretation of their faith.

Shi'a Muslims have a different call to prayer and do not practise prayer in the same way. Often they have three rather than five calls to prayer in a day. They will place on their foreheads a piece of hard clay from the Shi'a holy city of Karbala, in Iraq. They even add to the *shahadah* an addendum which reflects their beliefs, reciting 'There is no God but Allah and Muhammad is the messenger of Allah, Ali is the friend of Allah, the successor of the Messenger of Allah and his first caliph.' They also give preference to a different set of *Hadith*, namely those narrated by Ali and Fatima.

exclusive, but both Sunni and Shi'a can practise Sufism as a way of exploring the inner life and spirituality. It takes its name from a term for wool, 'suf'.

A suf was someone who wore wool and who in early Islam was regarded as living a simple life dedicated to living in the presence of God. Poetry is important in Sufism and is thought to express the deepest desires of the heart and the union of the soul with God. The notion of the immanence rather than the transcendence of God is important. God is not divorced from the world, but his presence lives within it. *Sufis* and *Suffiyas*, as female followers of the path are called, stress self-discipline and self-denial. They follow spiritual practices that they believe lead them to greater realms of union with God.

Wahhabism

The Wahhabis trace their origins back to Muhammad ibn 'Abd al-Wahhab, who in 1740 established a reformation of the form of Islam then practised within the Arabian peninsula. Regarded as a very conservative path within Islam, Wahhabism is still the predominant form of Islam within Saudi Arabia. It rejects accommodation with modern culture and is disdainful of Sufi practices, which it regards as mysticism. It disagrees with any veneration of tombs and of seeking intercession from those considered to be Islamic saints. It does not

Shi'a Muslim men lift their palms during Friday noon prayers in the southern holy city of Karbala, 110 km (68.3 miles) from Baghdad.

accept any innovation and seeks a return to the pure practices advocated by the Qur'an.

Sacred Writings

The Muslim holy book is called the Qur'an. It is an extremely important text within Islam and many learn it entirely by heart. Many Muslim children attend special schools and classes where the sole focus is the memorizing and recitation of the Qur'an.

Another group of writings, the *Hadith*, are also very influential within Islam, but they do not have the same status as the Qur'an. The *Hadith* are collections of Muhammad's teachings.

The Qur'an

The root of the word 'Qur'an' implies reading and the recitation of what has been read. It is believed that the words of the Qur'an were given directly to Muhammad by God and were then recorded. It is considered to be a special revelation that shows forth a unique and timeless God, who upholds the universe by his power.

The Qur'an is believed to explain the place of the human being within the whole created order. Its central message is that God is transcendent and that he is above all else and at the centre of all existence. It was originally compiled in Arabic and it is this Arabic text that is considered the most sacred and the one that should be used, although Muslims who do not speak or read Arabic are permitted to have a copy of the sacred book in their own language. Any vernacular copy, however, is regarded as a commentary on the Arabic version rather than having the full status accorded to the Arabic version.

◆ The Qur'an is divided into chapters, each chapter being called a *surah*.

◆ There are 114 *surahs* in all, consisting of in excess of 6,600 verses.

◆ The longest *surah* is *Surah* 2, which has 286 verses.

◆ The shortest is *Surah* 103, which has only three verses.

◆ With the exception of *Surah* 9, all of them begin with the words: 'In the name of Allah, most gracious, most merciful.'

The Qur'an divides the revelation to Muhammad into two distinct sections. One deals with the revelations he received at Mecca, which are known as the *Meccan Surahs*, the other with the revelations in Medina, the *Medina Surahs*.

◆ The *Meccan Surahs* tell of a Muhammad who is confronting evil. They tell of reward and punishment according to deeds done. They deal with the issue of the human heart and emotions.

◆ The *Medina Surahs* – reflecting a time when Muhammad was establishing his community and was attempting to create a settled society – deal with matters of order, mutual existence, laws, social and personal relationships, marriage, war, and daily work.

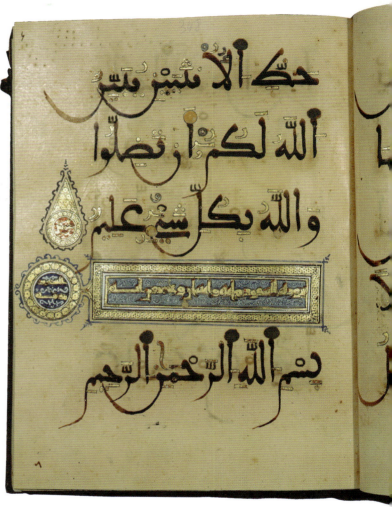

A page from a 13th-century Qur'an manuscript, showing *Surah* 13, verse 176.

Opposite: Iranian clerical students study in the courtyard of the Grand Ayatollah Saafi Golpayegani religious school in Iran's clerical capital, Qom, 120 km (74.5 miles) south of Tehran.

The Qur'an in wider society

The Qur'an teaches that there is no separation between the secular and the sacred realms. As a result, it offers guidance on a vast array of topics, covering not only religious themes, but also matters of law, ethics, exhortation, community building, and advice. It has many mystical themes and it expresses its message not only in concrete terms, but in the form of parable and allegorical stories. It focuses strongly on the mercy of God and on the concept of divine forgiveness. Justice, both social and personal, is an important issue that is addressed in Sufism. It teaches that many aspects of God are mysterious to human beings and cannot be understood.

The Qur'an in daily life

Many Muslims read the Qur'an daily. It regulates all individual and collective behaviour. It is kept at a height above the Muslim, never on the floor, and is usually placed on a special shelf or table, wrapped in a cloth.

The Qur'an is subject to a law of interpretation known as the doctrine of abrogation. This recognizes that certain verses abrogate or replace other verses. In other words, where a contradiction occurs, a later verse may be understood as replacing an earlier one, since circumstances in the community or situation may have changed.

Muslims accept other religious writings, such as the Torah (or *Tawrat* as Muslims refer to it), the Psalms or *Zabur* and the gospel or *Injil*. However, in Muslim theology the Qur'an supersedes all of these. Adam, Abraham, Moses, David,

and Jesus are all accepted as prophets whose teachings are to be respected, but Muhammad is the final and most important prophet.

The Hadith

The crucial difference between the Qur'an and the *Hadith* – which are collections of Muhammad's teachings and of course influential – is that the former is believed to have come directly from God. The *Hadith* are regarded as the words of either Muhammad or his close companions and as such are very valuable in gaining a fuller understanding of the Qur'an. There are many books which make up the *Hadith*.

Core Beliefs

Every aspect of Islamic life is built upon the foundation of monotheistic faith. The belief in the oneness of God and the place of the Prophet Muhammad are absolutely fundamental in setting the scene for all other aspects of Muslim faith. Owing to the non-separation of the secular and the sacred, Muslim belief permeates every aspect of existence.

The centrality of the law of God

One of the most powerful conduits for this all-permeating belief is the area of *Shari'a*. *Shari'a* regulates every area of Muslim daily life. It is essentially a legal code, but in reality it is much more. It also regulates and directs the Muslim inner life and attitudes. *Shari'a* is based on the Qur'an but it draws much of its content from the *Hadith*. It also relies on legal interpretation

Islamic Law

In the first two centuries of the development of Islam, a legal system began to be formed which had as its formative influences both the authority of the Qur'an and the sayings and actions of the Prophet as passed down in tradition. Very quickly this system of Islamic law, known as *Shari'a,* established itself as the most important institution in Islam.[1]

Shari'a literally means 'the way to the water hole'. This encompasses the idea of Islamic law showing the right path in life, the path which will bring ultimate joy and peace. *Shari'a* is not simply a code of law, but the guide to a way of life, to the correct way of living. It has a divine origin and God is the only one who can legislate for humankind.

Those scholars who interpreted the law, the Islamic jurists or *ulema*, gained a great deal of influence owing to their role in guiding Islamic daily practice and setting legal principles. The various schools of law formed by these jurists presented a variety of interpretations and expressions of Islamic practice.

◆ The *Hanifite* school interprets the law in a way which many consider to be quite liberal, allowing a wider role and authority to the considered opinion of scholars. It is most prevalent in Iraq, Iran, Pakistan, and India.

◆ The *Malikite* school, followed in eastern Arabia, North Africa, and some areas of Egypt gives particular attention to the opinions of the communities in which it holds sway.

◆ The *Shafi'ite* school gives no place to the authority of opinion and appeals primarily to the authority of the *Hadith*. This school of thought is found in Cairo, the southern parts of Arabia, India, and Indonesia.

◆ The *Hanbalite* school of *Shari'a* is very conservative, has no place for opinion and subordinates the *Hadith* to the Qur'an. It is influential in Saudi Arabia.

given by respected Islamic theologians and scholars. Most mosques will have an *imam*, a religious leader or teacher who will guide decision-making when there is a point of dispute about *Shari'a* or where the law appears unclear. Within Muslim countries the application of *Shari'a* can vary considerably. In some places, particularly in Saudi Arabia, the exercise of *Shari'a* often leads to restrictions and punishments which are foreign to the mind of the non-Muslim, particularly in the West.

Holy sites in Mecca

In Mecca it is the Ka'ba that becomes the main centre for gathering. Pilgrims walk around the cube-shaped 'House of God' believed by Muslims to have been built by the prophet Abraham and his son Ishmael.

Set in one of the corners of the Ka'ba is the black stone believed to have been given to Abraham directly from God through the angel Gabriel. The Ka'ba is roughly 14 metres high, 10 metres wide and 15 metres long. It is situated in a mosque in the centre of Mecca. The Ka'ba itself is covered in a black cloth, embroidered with verses of the Qur'an in gold thread. It is this structure which Muslims face when they turn towards Mecca in prayer.

Pilgrims make seven circuits of the Ka'ba, walking anti-clockwise. They must remain pure while on pilgrimage and should abstain from wearing jewellery and from any sexual activity. Everyone wears white. During the pilgrimage, pilgrims will also visit the *zamzam* well, where it is believed God raised up a spring of water for Hagar – the servant of Abraham

The Five Pillars of Islam

The Five Pillars of Islam most clearly demonstrate the focus on the oneness of God. The pillars outline the five primary areas of religious practice which a Muslim must follow. The first of the pillars is basically a statement of faith which sets the rest in context.

1 Shahadah

The *Shahadah* or declaration of faith reminds the Muslim that, 'There is no God but Allah and Muhammad is the messenger of Allah.' It is a simple-sounding statement that reflects a profound spiritual reality. It is this declaration which must be made for someone to become a Muslim. It is divided into two essential concepts.

First, it affirms absolute monotheism.

Secondly, it underlines the central part played by Muhammad by highlighting the belief that he is the giver of God's revelation.

It is not simply a spoken formula, or something to which the Muslim gives mere lip service. It must be rooted in the heart of the Muslim and must come from a conviction and a belief in its affirmation. It should be recited in Arabic, where it reads, 'La ilaha 'illa 'llah Muhammadun rasulu 'ikh.' Muhammad is regarded as the last prophet in a line of prophets that has its origin in Adam. The revelation mediated by Muhammad is the final revelation. It supersedes all others.

2 Salat

The second pillar, *Salat*, is prayer. Muslims pray five times a day: at sunrise, noon, mid-afternoon, sunset and evening. The position of *Salat* straight after the *Shahadah* indicates the importance attached to it. Prayer is the response to this one God and is his proper due. It underlines the relationship between God and his creation. Creation responds to its creator in prayer.

A familiar sound in the Middle East and in Muslim countries is the sound of the *muezzin* calling the faithful to prayer from the top of a tower above the mosque, known as a minaret. The call goes out, 'Allahu Akbar'– 'God is most great.' Before a Muslim prays, the body is cleansed and this cleansing is a sign of purity that is not only physical, but spiritual and mental as well.

Salat prayers are formal prayers, as distinct from *du'ah*, which are petitionary prayers and are done privately or at times outside the set periods. The cleansing is known as *wudhu*. While it is taking place, the believer utters the prayer: 'In the name of God the Beneficient, the Merciful.' Muslims will pray wherever they are, even if they are travelling. If they are at home, they will face Mecca and pray. If outside the home, they will find a quiet place and pray there. Often a Muslim will take a light prayer mat and will use this to kneel upon. Prayer is always said facing the direction of the holy city of Mecca.

When possible Muslims will respond to the call to prayer and pray in the mosque. Again, the mosque congregation will face Mecca to recite the prayers, led by either an *imam* or another senior person. Prayer in the mosque involves movements that indicate reverence and submission. Muslims will bow, kneel, or prostrate themselves at various times. Noontime prayer on Friday, the Muslim holy day, is usually the time for congregational prayer and during this time of prayer a sermon will be preached.

3 Zakat

Almsgiving, *zakat*, is the third pillar. The Muslim undertakes to express devotion to God through giving to the people of God. Muslims are expected to know and take care of the social and economic needs of their local communities. *Zakat* is not a tax on income, but on accumulated wealth and assets. If wealth is accumulated for purely selfish means, that is condemned by the Qur'an. Those who are blessed by God with economic well-being are expected to help those who are not as financially secure.

Zakat is not just an act of charity. It is a requirement. But it is not just a physical act, it is primarily a spiritual one and it reflects the attitudes of the heart and one's attitude towards money and material things. It is also a way in which Muslims can view themselves as being part of a wider community (*ummah*), whether they give or receive.

4 Sawm

The fourth pillar is fasting or *sawm*. The Muslim is expected to fast during the holy month of *Ramadan*. *Ramadan* is observed in the ninth month of the Islamic lunar calendar. The daily fast during this month lasts from dawn to dusk. Healthy Muslims must abstain from all food, drink and sex. The fast is observed until sunset. Muslims who want to eat something before the day begins must rise before dawn to eat a meal known as the *suhoor*.

Muslims try not to focus their attention so much on the fast as on the spiritual benefits that flow from it. *Ramadan* is a time of spiritual discipline, soul-searching and self-denial, which fasting enables. It is believed in Islam and in many other religious traditions that fasting opens up the spiritual nature and enables the human being to focus on the inner life through the denial of the outer one.

The fast takes place at a different time each year, owing to the adoption of the lunar calendar. When *Ramadan* falls in hot months, it makes the fast even more difficult, as the believer must abstain from drinking any liquid. Those who are old or infirm, young children, pregnant women and those who have to go on a long and tiresome journey are exempted from fasting. Muslims celebrate one of the most important events in the life of Muhammad during *Ramadan*, the *Night of Power*, when Muhammad received the first vision. The final ten days of *Ramadan*, during which time the *Night of Power* is remembered, are the most important days of the whole fast period. The month of *Ramadan* ends with a three-day festival, *'Id-al-Fitr* (see p. 68).

5 Hajj

The fifth pillar is based on the theme of pilgrimage or *hajj*. Pilgrimage is an important feature in many world faiths. In Islam, as in other religions, it symbolizes the believer's journey through life. The essential element of the *hajj* in Muslim belief is that it must take place in Mecca. It need only be made once in a lifetime, but many do it as often as they can as an act of spiritual worship and as a statement of belief.

The season of pilgrimages normally follows the time of fasting, *Ramadan*. It must be undertaken if one is financially able to do so. Those who cannot go to Mecca because of ill health or financial need are able to fulfil *hajj* by doing something that symbolizes their journey towards God in some way. This may involve an act of charity or self-sacrifice.

The communal aspect of *hajj* is important to Muslims. The feeling of unity gained from thousands of pilgrims travelling to Mecca at the same time creates a strong sense of the inter-relatedness of all members of the faith.

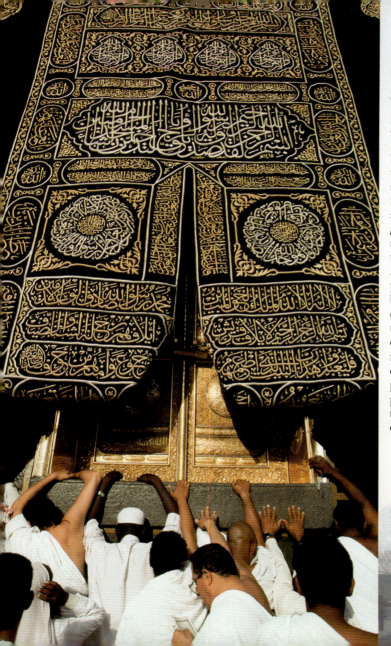

with whom he conceived Ishmael – when Hagar and Ishmael faced death in the desert. Muslims also visit the Plain of Arafat, where Muhammad preached his last sermon. There they seek forgiveness for sin. The pilgrimage ends with *'Id-al-Adha*, the Feast of Sacrifice (see below).

The Muslim belief in the giving of the black stone of the *Ka'ba* to Abraham by the angel Gabriel, or *Jibril*, is evidence of another important area of Islam, the belief in angels. Angels are believed to be servants and messengers of God. The Qur'an was given to Muhammad through the agency of an angel. Angels also have the responsibility to point Muslims to a belief in judgment. A Day of Judgment will come, Islam preaches. Human beings will be judged according to the extent they have conformed to God's *Shari'a*. The place of reward, the heavenly realm, will be a place of unrivalled bliss and peace. Hell, the place of punishment, is a place of torture and deep regret for evildoing.

Worship and festivals

In its character and conduct, Muslim worship is first and foremost a communal affair. Even when conducted in private, all Muslims are joined together by their mutual bond of devotion to one God and the all-important centre of prayer, the holy city of Mecca.

The mosque

Muslims use a mosque as their place of worship. Its name derives from the Arabic term *masjid*, which means 'to prostrate'. The mosque, therefore, is the place where the follower of Islam truly shows submission to God and this is physically expressed in the acts of bowing and prostrating. The mosque is the very centre of the Muslim community. It is primarily a place of prayer and worship, but it will also house administrative centres, education areas and rooms used for community activities. If the mosque is big enough and significant enough, the *imam* and his family might live there. Mosques are usually rectangular and will often contain an area where ritual washing can take place. Worshippers will wash their feet, hands and faces prior to entering the mosque to pray. They will also remove their shoes. In many countries, but especially in Muslim countries, the mosque will have a tower or minaret. From on high will go forth the call to prayer, uttered by the *muezzin,* whose responsibility it is to remind the community to turn their faces towards Mecca. The *qibla* wall inside the mosque will show the believer the direction to Mecca.

The inside of the mosque is normally plain and carpeted. Often, however, it will be decorated with elaborate Arabic script. Any representation of God or Muhammad is forbidden.

Left: A few pilgrims are fortunate to stop at the door of the Ka'ba in Mecca, the focus of Muslim prayer. The black cloth covering the Ka'ba is called a *kiswah,* and is embroidered with Qur'anic verses.

Background: The rooftops and minarets of Istanbul.

The leader of prayer in the mosque will conduct the mosque services from a raised pulpit or *minbar*. Prayer is conducted five times a day. The prayer times are actually more like prayer periods. Prayer at the mosque is at set times, but individuals who are following the ritual of morning prayer (*fajr*), noonday prayer (*zuhr*), mid-afternoon prayer (*'asr*), prayer at sunset (*maghrib*) and night prayer (*'isha*) may not be able to respond to the call immediately and so have a period of grace, lasting about two hours, in which they can pray.

In Muslim homes, believers will use special mats to kneel upon and when a Muslim is travelling a light prayer mat may be brought along to facilitate daily observance. Praying communally in the mosque, Muslims will stand in long lines and pray in unison, bowing and prostrating and standing at various times.

Festivals

Muslims observe many festivals through the year.

◆ *Muharram* is the Muslim New Year and celebrates the journey of Muhammad to Medina, the *hijrah*. It is regarded as the festival that commemorates the very beginning of the Muslim faith.

◆ *Milad-al-Nabi* in the third month of the Muslim calendar is the feast day to honour the birth of the Prophet Muhammad. Sunni Muslims celebrate the event on the twelfth of the month and Shi'a Muslims on the seventeenth.

◆ *Ramadan* is a period of strict abstention from food and drink, when prayer is

said fervently and when those who have wandered from regular observance are able to renew their commitment. The religious observance during *Ramadan* highlights its role as the most important festival of the year.

◆ *'Id-al-Fitr* is a time of feasting to mark the end of *Ramadan*. The fast is broken and people wear their best clothes to gather in large groups – at home or elsewhere – to give each other gifts and enjoy specially prepared meals.

◆ *'Id-al-Adha* (the Feast of Sacrifice or Ritual Slaughter) recalls the time when God put Abraham to the test by instructing him to sacrifice his son Ishmael. (In Jewish and Christian tradition it is the other son, Isaac, who is believed to be the potential sacrifice.) In view of the belief that God then substituted a ram for Ishmael and sacrificed it instead, animals are sacrificed at *'Id-al-Adha* and their meat is either eaten or given to the poor. The festival takes place after the pilgrimage season, the time of *hajj*, and is a time for families to celebrate together.

Family and Society

As societies in the West have become liberated from traditions that restricted people in how they could legally behave, there has been a decrease in the percentage of couples getting married in church or marrying at all and an increase in the number of one-parent families. Within Islam the family continues to be of very great

Top right: Women wearing burquas in Charikar, Afghanistan.

Far right: A young Muslim woman wears a long hijab.

mind, but it is considered within these societies to be a wise way to conduct the arrangement. It builds an alliance between two families and the couple are thought to benefit from the collective wisdom and advice of parents and extended families. Marriage is not considered to be a sacramental affair, but rather a social and civil partnership. In some Muslim communities, a man is permitted to marry more than one wife. The injunction is placed on him to treat all his wives equally. If he cannot, he should marry only one. The custom arose as a result of many widows being left without any means of support following the Battle of Uhud, which was fought in 625 CE. Polygamy provided the solution. Many Muslims think that this was an exceptional situation and that the custom should not prevail today.

Divorce is allowed in Islam. However, in a society that places such emphasis on marriage, as with Jews and Christians, a couple would be expected to do everything possible to avoid this split. Muslims believe God hates divorce, but it has been allowed because of human weakness and failing.

importance. As a result, there is a strong emphasis on marriage.

Marriage and the family

Marriage is a bond between two individuals, but the significance of this is greatly widened within Islam because, in marriage, two families join together as well. It is within the family that the Muslim child and young person is able to be shaped and inducted in Islamic values and the Islamic way of life. The family is a nurturing unit, but it is a teaching unit as well. Large parts of the Qur'an are given over to teaching on the subject of marriage. All sexual activity is expected to take place within marriage; extramarital relationships are strictly discouraged. In Muslim societies severe penalties may be imposed for fornication or adultery.

In many Muslim communities, marriages may be arranged. Such a practice can seem alien to the Western

Women and Islam

The position of women in Islam is controversial. Muslims point out that, prior to Muhammad's teaching,

Islam in the West

The relationship between Islam and the West[2] has often been characterized by conflict and confrontation. In more contemporary times the image of Islam in the West has been overshadowed by acts of terrorism by a tiny minority that taint the reputation of all Muslims. In such an atmosphere, the missionary efforts of Islam in the Western world are presented with significant challenges.

Most Muslims believe the Qur'an teaches that mission is an important part of the spread of the faith. Some even believe in the eventual conversion of the West to Islam, although this is not a universal aspiration within Islam.

When Westerners do convert to Islam, they give as one reason for their conversion dissatisfaction with the prevailing ideologies of the West. This dissatisfaction is directed not only against the religious institutions but also against secular society and what is seen as an almost irredeemable drift towards immorality. Viewing Islam as encompassing a unified philosophy of life, some Westerners turn to it for what they believe to be considered answers to the problems posed by living in the modern world. The attention given within Islam to ethical and moral issues is particularly attractive. Many are also drawn to Sufi mysticism, which provides them with a mystical religious path that they find difficult to locate within Western religious systems, which are often characterized by an overemphasis on the rational and empirical.

women were severely ill-treated on the Arabian peninsula and in surrounding nations and that Islam accorded them dignity and respect. The wearing of what is seen as restrictive dress is a major issue for debate, with Western women in particular, and many Islamic women, viewing the restrictions imposed by the *hijab*, *chador*, and *burqua* as a breach of human rights and a method of imposing control. On the other hand, many Muslim women would insist that covering their bodies and faces frees them from sexual advances and from being viewed as sexual objects.

Contemporary Issues

Muslim countries, and Muslim minorities within other countries, are under pressure from within and without. One of the most pressing issues between the Muslim and non-Muslim world is that, in the West, the view of Islam that prevails is a caricature of the faith, based on a simplistic perception originating from the belief that Islam is a religion of terror rather than of peace. Some Muslims may regard continued Western military presence in the Middle East as frightening evidence of a reborn medieval crusade. Nonetheless, they have to deal with a recent phenomenon known as Islamophobia, a fear of Islam and of all things connected with the faith.

Islam and terror

The term 'Islamophobia' gained particular resonance following the events of 11 September 2001 when, claiming to act in the name of Islam, terrorists crashed airliners into two iconic skyscrapers in New York. The vast majority of Muslims throughout the world were horrified by this murderous act, supposedly committed in their name, and it was condemned by many prominent Muslim leaders. Nevertheless, the majority is being called upon to acknowledge the reality of – and deal with – the presence of those within the faith who would advance their cause by means of terrorist violence.

The resulting horror and debate has

served to highlight severe divisions between Islam and Western societies in particular, with all Muslims being tarnished by the actions of a few. 'Islamic terrorism' has now become a phrase heard widely in the media and Muslim communities in the West have found themselves increasingly isolated in the wake of what is termed a 'clash of civilizations'. Within Islam itself, a deep and complicated debate is taking place as to what it means to be a Muslim in the twenty-first century and how Muslims should relate to the other cultures around them. Political and religious ferment within major Islamic world centres, such as Iraq, Iran, Pakistan, Saudi Arabia, and Afghanistan serves to further inflame relationships with the West, with increasing talk of 'radicalized' Islam and 'extremism'.

The challenges of secularism

Muslim societies are facing the challenges of secularism and materialism and many Muslims are questioning traditional teachings and strictures. There is a wide degree of interpretation of the law in different Muslim societies with regard to the role and status of women. This is seen as one of the most pressing contemporary issues facing Islam. In many Muslim societies women have become greatly empowered, highly educated and extremely politicized, with women running for political office and holding significant positions of power. In other areas, women are not even allowed to drive cars or wear any form of westernized dress.

In light of the serious debates being conducted within Islam itself, and with the crisis of Islam's relationship with the West and other non-Muslim societies, the religion finds itself potentially at one of the most challenging, yet creative, periods in its history.

Reading guide to Islam

Ahmed, Akbar S., *Living Islam: From Samarkand to Stornoway*, Penguin Books and BBC Worldwide Ltd, London, 1995 edn.

Cook, Michael, *The Koran: A Very Short Introduction*, Oxford University Press, Oxford, 2000.

Esack, Farid, *The Qur'an: A User's Guide*, Oneworld, Oxford, 2007 edn.

Esposito, John L., *Islam: The Straight Path*, Oxford University Press, Oxford, 2005, revised third edn.

Guillaume, Alfred, *Islam*, Penguin Books, London, 1990 edn.

Kung, Hans, *Islam: Past, Present and Future*, Oneworld, Oxford, 2007.

Nelson, Kristian, *The Art of Reciting the Qur'an*, The American University in Cairo Press, Cairo and New York, 2002 edn.

Pargeter, Alison, *The New Frontiers of Jihad: Radical Islam in Europe*, I. B. Tauris, London, New York, 2008.

Rippin, Andrew, *Muslims: Their Religious Beliefs and Practices*, Routledge, London, 2005 edn.

Sonn, Tamara, *A Brief History of Islam*, Blackwell Publishing, Oxford, UK and Victoria, Australia, 2004.

Voll, John Obert, *Islam: Continuity and Change in the Modern World,* Syracuse University Press, New York, 1994, second edn.

Waines, David, *An Introduction to Islam*, Cambridge University Press, Cambridge, UK, 2004, second edn.

Zoroastrianism

History and Development

The origins of Zoroastrianism are centred in ancient Persia (modern Iran) where the faith developed for more than a thousand years before the founding of Islam.

Size Estimates vary enormously, from a long-accepted 200,000 adherents to a recent re-evaluation, still under review, which would make Zoroastrianism the world's seventeenth largest religion.

Founder The prophet Zarathushtra, also known as Zoroaster, (probably c. 1200 BCE). He was a priest and visionary who lived in what is now Iran.

Location Originating in ancient Persia among Indo-Iranians (or Aryans) and spreading to India (particularly around Mumbai) with significant modern communities in North America and Britain.

There has been considerable debate as to when Zoroastrianism was born. Scholars now tend to favour between 1500 BCE and 1000 BCE, perhaps 1200 BCE. Exact dating is difficult because Zoroastrianism was already an ancient faith when written records first began.

Origins in Persia

Zoroastrianism became the state religion of Iran's last great pre-Islamic empire. Its adoption as their religion by the Persian kings greatly increased its influence. A key figure in the expansion of the Persian empire in the centuries following the death of Zarathushtra was Cyrus (558–530 BCE). This ruler of the first Persian empire (at that time the world's largest empire) presided over a great territory in which faiths of various persuasions could prosper, and

during his reign Zoroastrianism became the empire's state religion.

A lasting influence

The priests of Zoroastrianism were known as *Magi* (the title given in the Bible to the wise men from the East who journeyed to see the infant Jesus, Matthew 2:1–12). They had an important role in developing and spreading the faith. By the time the second great Persian empire, the Sasanian empire, emerged in 224 CE, Zoroastrianism was well established, but the Sasanians cemented it further by building many religious centres and temples where the faith could be taught.

Zoroastrianism became a very powerful religious force across the region and remained so until the rise of Islam. It is claimed that Zoroastrianism contributed to the development of many of the major faiths. Judaism, Christianity, Islam, and even Mahayana Buddhism are all believed to have been influenced by it to some degree. Zoroastrians who settled in India in the early eighth century CE were the forerunners of the Parsi community there.

Founder and Significant Figures

The prophet Zarathushtra, who lived in ancient Persia, now Iran, was known to the Greeks as Zoroaster. This version of his name continues to be used in the West and the term Zoroastrianism has been derived from it.

Zarathushtra

The prophet was from an area that is now north-east Iran and south-west Afghanistan and was once part of southern Russia. A descendant of Indo-Iranians, also known as Aryans, he grew up in a noble family. He became a priest, married and had children. At the age of thirty he began to have visions. He had become interested in the nature of good and evil, and his visions were concerned with these twin issues.

Zarathushtra became aware that there was one true God, whose name was Ahura Mazda (the Wise Lord). He was a good and

Ahura Mazda, the supreme god in Zoroastrianism, is depicted in this monument at the UNESCO World Heritage Site, Persepolis, Iran.

The Ateshgah temple in Surakhany, Azerbaijan, the last Zoroastrian temple in the region, is lit up at night by the eternal sacred flame which has burned on the spot as far back as the 6th century. The current structure dates from the 18th century, but it was originally built over a pocket of natural gas that was vented to provide an eternal sacred fire. The sacred fire is considered to be a living, glowing symbol representing the energy and presence of God.

bountiful God who had created all things. Importantly, this God was a personal God. However, from the beginning Ahura Mazda had an adversary, known as Angra Mainyu, an evil spirit. Zarathushtra's visions continued for some ten years. At first he was disregarded and even persecuted. He made an important breakthrough when he converted King Vishtaspa. Once the king was converted, his household quickly followed him in accepting Zarathushtra's religion and eventually the king's subjects began to follow his example. Zarathushtra is reputed to have continued his priestly ministry until the age of seventy-seven. Zoroastrians believe that he died as a result of war.

Branches of Zoroastrianism

In modern times the followers of Zoroastrianism have declined in number. Worldwide, it has generally been thought that there are fewer than 200,000 believers in existence today, although some recent, unconfirmed estimates raise the possibility that there has been substantial undercounting. These followers of the religion are based mainly in India and Iran, but there are also important communities of Zoroastrians in North America, Britain, and Australia. There is a significant Zoroastrian community around the area of Mumbai in India, and some writers estimate the number of believers in that area at between 65,000 and 75,000. Zoroastrians are also to be found in Pakistan.

Zoroastrians in Iran

Iran's Zoroastrian community has endured much persecution and as a result has dwindled. It is estimated that about 25,000 remain, mainly in the capital, Teheran, and in the area of Yazdi. Between 1945 and 1965 many Zoroastrians moved to the capital from the more rural area of Yazdi and the Zoroastrian population of Yazdi halved.

During the 1960s Iranian Zoroastrians undertook reform of their practices, which resulted in the loss of many traditional rituals. Decline in the number of priests available affected both the rural and urban communities, but it gave opportunities to lay people to take up important roles. Following the revolution of 1979 life became quite difficult for Zoroastrians throughout Iran and numbers fell rapidly.

Parsis and Iranis

The term 'Parsi' refers to the community of Zoroastrians in India. Modern Parsis are descendants of Iranian Zoroastrians who settled in India more than 1,000 years ago. They settled originally in Gujarat and grew in influence. During the British presence in India the Parsis were strongly influenced by British cultural values. This had an effect on the community's adherence to its faith traditions and many Parsis lost touch with their cultural and religious past. This loss of identity has been further exacerbated by intermarriage with non-Parsis and in recent decades many have lost the knowledge of their religious customs and heritage. There are signs of a modest revival, however, with more interest being shown in the ancient customs in recent years, coupled with an increase in interest in the Zoroastrian priesthood. Zoroastrian authorities have been making strong efforts to provide accessible education in the faith.

The term 'Irani' refers to those Iranian Zoroastrians who have more recently moved to India, following persecution in Iran from the eighteenth century on.

Khshnumists

In the early twentieth century a religious movement grew from Parsi roots known as Khshnumism or *Ilm-e-Khshnum*, translated as 'Knowledge of Joy' or 'Science of spiritual satisfaction'. This was founded by Behramshah Shroff (1858–1927), a Parsi of Mumbai. Shroff claimed to have visited spiritual 'Masters' at Mount Demavand in Iran who enabled him to achieve enlightenment. In 1923 Shroff laid the foundations for a fire-temple in Mumbai that was finally consecrated in 2001.

Khshnumist teaching is theosophical in nature and there are links in teaching between *Ilm-e-Khshnum* and the Theosophical Society of the late nineteenth century, in which Parsis were involved. Khshnumists teach that the soul can be released from its bonds by a life of asceticism and vegetarianism. The soul can progress through birth and rebirth until it reaches the penultimate point of its journey. Just before its final release it is born into Zoroastrianism, which prepares it for the final stage.

Sacred Writings

Zoroastrianism was in existence as a faith long before writing was used. Its early history was therefore transmitted orally. The collection of holy texts eventually committed to writing is known as the Avesta. It was only finally compiled in written form during the reign of the Sasanians (226–651 CE) and it ran to twenty-one volumes. Following several invasions and wars, these copies were lost and what survives now is really only a portion of the original scriptures.

The Avesta

The language of this holy book, known as Avestan, could be understood and interpreted only by the priests of Zoroastrianism. The Avesta includes:

◆ seventeen hymns known as the *Gathas*, which are thought to have been composed by Zarathushtra himself;

◆ the *Yasna Haptanhaiti*, which sets out a ritual of liturgical worship;

◆ the *Visperand*, a text used to honour the lords or *Ahuras* within Zoroastrianism;

◆ the *Yashts* or hymns of praise;

◆ the *Vindedad*, a ritual which is used against demons.

Later texts

Around the ninth and tenth centuries CE many volumes were written that attempted to capture some of the essence of the original Avesta. These are basically commentaries and summaries or translations of books which have been lost, but they are not entirely reliable. They are written in Middle Persian, or Pahlavi.

Core Beliefs

Warfare was common in the society in which Zarathushtra lived, and this led Zarathushtra to meditate deeply on matters of good and evil. As a result of his visions he taught that a wise, good, and uncreated God, Ahura Mazda, the Lord of Wisdom, was opposed by another uncreated being, an evil spirit known as Angra Mainyu (or Ahriman in Middle Persian).

The cosmic battle

In order to destroy the evil Angra Mainyu, Zarathushtra believed, Ahura Mazda created the physical world to be a place where a great cosmic battle could take place between the forces of good and the forces of evil. Ahura Mazda dwelt in light, served by six divine, spiritual beings – the 'Holy Immortals' or *Amesha Spentas*. These six, along with Ahura Mazda's Holy Spirit, Spenta Mainyu, functioned as intermediaries between Ahura Mazda and creation itself.

Each *Amesha Spenta* is an aspect of God but also an individual being in and of itself. Their individual names indicate their spirituality:

◆ Vohu Manah or 'Good Mind or Purpose'

◆ Asha Vahishta or 'Best Righteousness'

◆ Armaiti or 'Holy Devotion'

Zoroastrian worshippers pray at the ancient Chak Chak temple which is built in the mountains in a deserted area, some 110 km (68.3 miles) north of the central Iranian city of Yazd. The Zoroastrians celebrate their annual religious Chakchak festival with a pilgrimage to the deserted site, which lasts five days.

◆ Khshathra Vairya or 'Desirable Dominion'

◆ Haurvatat or 'Health'

◆ Ameretat or 'Immortality'.

Each of the *Amesha Spentas* has a specific function within the seven realms of creation, which are sky, water, earth, plants, cattle, humanity, and fire. Through them Ahura Mazda can be present in the totality of the created order while himself remaining transcendent. The role of the *Amesha Spentas* is to fight against evil within their own realms. Zarathushtra believed that the created order was in itself good, since it was created by God and was infused with the presence of a God who was both transcendent and immanent. All evil had its origin in Angra Mainyu.

Humans have to make a choice in their lives: to follow good or evil. After death they will face judgment and their soul needs to pass over a chasm on the 'Bridge of the Separator' or Chinvat bridge. If the good deeds of their lives outweigh the bad, the bridge becomes a broad route to eternal happiness with Ahura Mazda. If the

77

Zoroastrian ethical teaching

Zoroastrianism is a profoundly ethical religion with a very strong emphasis on the battle between good and evil. Zoroastrian morality is expressed in the words *humat*, *hukht*, and *huvarsht*. These respectively stand for good thoughts, good words, and good deeds. The most important of the three is *huvarsht* or good deeds.

Moderation is an important concept within Zoroastrianism and underpins the faith's moral teachings. Stress is placed on the avoidance of extremes in any area of life. Wisdom enables humankind to act in a moderate way. Wisdom or *khrat* is best understood as common sense. Life is there to be enjoyed, but extremes will lead to pain and suffering. Therefore all things should be enjoyed in moderation and the human being should be conscious of the considerations of the next life.

Zoroastrian thinking on moderation is well expressed in the Book of the Spirit of Wisdom or *Mnk i Khrat*, possibly published in the sixth century CE.

"All men should become sober by drinking wine in moderation. For these several benefits accrue to a man through the drinking of wine in moderation. He digests his food and kindles the (digestive) fire. His wit and intelligence, seed and blood are increased, care is driven away, his colour is heightened, he remembers what he has forgotten, he makes room for goodness in his thoughts [...]. And these several defects appear in the man who drinks wine immoderately. His wit and intelligence, seed and blood decrease. He ruins his liver and stores up sickness (for himself); his colour fades and his strength and endurance fail."[1]

bad outweighs the good, then the bridge narrows and functions as a slippery route to eternal punishment with Angra Mainyu.

Zoroastrian eschatology

The aim of good is to bring about the defeat of evil. This is a lengthy process. At some time, which is difficult to specify – but which will be during a final period of history – three saviour figures are expected to emerge at different times of crisis. In each case, the seed of the prophet, preserved miraculously in a lake, impregnates a virgin and the saviours born as a result are tasked with the role of destroying a part of the evil forces. The third saviour figure, known as the Saoshyant, ushers in a last judgment which is preceded by a final cosmic battle between good and evil. The earth is transformed and renewed, human beings who have died are resurrected and their bodies and souls are reunited. They are assigned a final judgment and the souls of the good live with Ahura Mazda as part of this new, wholly good creation. Evil is finally defeated.

Worship and Festivals

Purity and cleanliness are important elements in all Zoroastrian ceremonies.

Sacred fire and purity

Fire is a central theme of Zoroastrian worship. It symbolizes purity. The Zoroastrian is expected to pray five times a day and fire must be involved. Purity is a key feature of the faith, and certain practices – such as walking barefoot, contact with blood or dirt or any other pollutant – render believers unclean and prevent them from praying. Therefore the believer must ritually wash before praying. Prayer is usually done standing up, during which the believer will untie and retie a sacred cord known as the *kusti*, which is worn constantly.

For more important events a more

The seven festivals

According to Zoroastrian teaching, Ahura Mazda rules over seven creations which together make up the entire world. To help in the task of defeating evil, Ahura Mazda initially ruled with six lesser divine beings, or *Amesha Spentas,* called into his service by his own Holy Spirit, *Spenta Mainyu.* The *Amesha Spentas* cooperated with other benign divine beings, known as the *Yazatas* or 'Beings worthy of worship'.

Zarathushtra expected his followers to observe seven particular festivals. These are known as the *gahambars* and are dedicated to Ahura Mazda and his helpers. Six of the festivals have a farming or pastoral focus, one is dedicated to fire.[2]

- *Maidhyoi-zaremaya* Mid-spring
- *Maidhyoi-shema* Mid-summer
- *Paitishahya* The Feast of bringing in the corn
- *Ayathrima* The Feast of homecoming or bringing in the cattle from their pastures
- *Maidhyairya* Mid-winter
- *Hamaspathmaedaya* A term of uncertain meaning, given to a feast celebrated on the last night of the year, before the spring equinox
- *No Ruz* The festival of 'New Day' honours the seventh creation of the world, fire. It celebrates the time when good will finally triumph over evil and lead to a 'New Day' or eternal happiness.

Each of the festivals is celebrated by the community attending religious services early in the day and then gathering to eat food together.

comprehensive ceremony of purification, a ritual bath known as a *nahn*, is undergone in the presence of a priest. Priests go through the *barashnom*, a very thorough cleansing as part of a nine-day retreat, before they are allowed to preside over ceremonies in the inner courts of the fire temples. Sacred fire is kept burning in the fire temples in a large vessel. Those entering for worship leave an offering of wood for the fire. Individual prayers are then made before the fire. The prayer room of a fire temple is devoid of any ornamentation and is kept scrupulously clean. The priest has a very important role in keeping the fire and priests come from priestly families. Because of the need for ritual purity, only Zoroastrians themselves can participate in ceremonies.

Children born into the faith are formally initiated between the ages of seven and nine. The child is given a sacred shirt and a sacred cord, the *sudreh* and *kusti*. These are worn for the rest of the Zoroastrian's life.

Above: Children perform the important Navjote ritual in Bombay, India. This ceremony is the ritual rite of passage for children to be accepted into the Parsi community. Here, a priest ties a sacred thread around the child's waist as he/she chants the Ahuna Vairya, the most ancient and powerful Masdayasan prayers.

Major holy days

Zoroastrians observe seven special holy days, the six *gahambars* and *No Ruz* or the 'New Day'. These celebrate the final vindication of good over evil. Other holy days indicate the importance of water and fire, *Aban Jashan* and *Adar Jashan*. Water and fire are especially honoured and care is taken not to extinguish the flame in the home or elsewhere, but to allow it to die by itself.

Family and Society

Because Zoroastrianism is such a small religious community, the family is even more important. It is necessary for the Parsis in India and the Zoroastrians in Iran to protect their distinct identities. Within Parsi households, women enjoy a lot of freedom and they are encouraged to succeed and do well. Both the Parsis and the Iranian Zoroastrians (Iranis) foster strong community spirit and many organizations have been founded to provide support.

In general, the Parsis have been more prosperous than the Iranis. The strength of the sense of identity in both groups can be discerned by the survival of the religion and its customs over such a long period of time, in spite of its relatively small numbers. Children are initiated into the faith and from this point are required to observe the rituals.

Weddings and funerals

Marriage is strongly encouraged and the priests marry as well. The marriage ceremony is regarded as having a sacred as well as a legal function. Funeral rites are particularly important. The body is washed, wrapped, and placed on a hard material, such as stone. In India and in Iran it is then carried to a round, roofless 'tower of silence' or *dakhma*, where it is left exposed to the vultures, who devour the flesh. In the West burial can take place, but it is the custom to encase the coffin in cement so that the soil is not made impure. Cremation is an acceptable alternative.

Contemporary Issues

Zoroastrians, either of Iranian descent or Parsi, have dispersed all over the world. The Parsis, in general, have done well in business, especially in East Africa. About 5,000 Zoroastrians are to be found in Britain and about 15,000 in North America. Most overseas Zoroastrians are of Parsi heritage, rather than Iranian. As a result Zoroastrians in Iran tend to have a stronger cultural identity, although they do suffer from more social discrimination.

A Parsi wedding celebration in a Bombay hotel.

In the outside world

There are reports that younger Zoroastrians are showing a renewed interest in their ancient faith and that this has been strengthened by the increase in profile of the religion as a whole. Zoroastrians are playing a greater role in inter-faith discussions.

There are dangers, particularly in North America, that the ritualistic aspect of Zoroastrianism is suffering as a result of a greater emphasis on the ethical and moral

Left: Iranian Zoroastrians dance around a fire during celebrations to commemorate Sade in Teheran. Sade is the day Zoroastrians believe fire was discovered. On the eleventh day of the eleventh month of the Iranian calendar, Sade marks the warming of the ground and the coming of spring.

From Bábism to Bahá'í

Bahá'u'lláh left many writings behind. In accordance with their message his followers built on the teachings of all the world's religions in order to bring about one great universal faith. Bahá'u'lláh was succeeded by his son, 'Abdu'l-Bahá, who continued to preach the message that Bahá'u'lláh was the saviour promised to the world, a saviour who would be the universal manifestation of divinity. Inspired by the leadership of Bahá'u'lláh, the movement once known as Bábism had evolved into Bahá'í.

Founder and Significant Figures

The Glory of God (1817–92)

Mirza Hussayn 'Ali Nuri was born in Teheran, the capital of modern-day Iran. From 1844 he was a fervent follower of the Báb, and after the Báb's death in 1850 he became a leading figure among the Bábis.

In 1852, in retaliation for the execution of the Báb, elements in Bábism planned to assassinate the shah. Mirza Hussayn 'Ali Nuri was implicated and thrown into prison. Released after four months he was exiled and found refuge in Baghdad. He quickly became Bábism's spokesman in both Iraq and Iran. On the basis of a number of spiritual and mystical experiences he claimed that he was a prophet and even a manifestation of God for the age in which he lived.

In 1863 he made his claim to be the Promised One (as foretold by the Báb) while on a journey to Constantinople,

The Báb (1819–50)

The Báb[1] was born as Sayyid 'Ali Muhammad Shirazi in Shiraz, an ancient cultural capital and city of poets (in modern-day Iran). His family was descended from the Prophet Muhammad. From an early age he showed a strong interest in religious matters. He engaged in pilgrimage to many of the Shi'ite holy sites in Iran and Iraq and became particularly devoted to teaching about the hidden, twelfth imam or *Mahdi* who would one day return and teach the world right from wrong.

Sayyid 'Ali Muhammad Shirazi began to be convinced that he had been chosen by God to fulfil a divine mission and he claimed for himself the title *báb* or 'gate'. The disciples who gathered around him were known as 'Bábis'. Many who heard their message began to believe the Báb might be the 'hidden imam', having returned. The followers of the young man saw him as a manifestation of God.

The claims divided public opinion and alarmed the government. The Báb's claim to be the 'hidden imam' could be interpreted as a political challenge to the authorities, since the idea of the return of the *Mahdi* was profoundly connected with the notion of rebellion and revolution. The Báb amended his claims. He stated that, while he was not a gate to knowledge of the 'hidden imam', he was a Gate of God. The furore over his claims did not die down and he was executed in 1850.

His cause was not helped by the activities of his followers while he was in prison. They travelled the country gaining converts even amongst the Muslim clergy, while being sharply opposed by other religious leaders. In 1848 the Bábi leaders declared the Báb to be not the *Mahdi* or 'twelfth imam', but rather a prophet sent in place of Muhammad. The government responded with crushing force to put down the unrest, resulting in the execution of the Bábi leaders, including the Báb.

to which he had been summoned by the leaders of the Ottoman empire. He was banished to Adrianople, where he suffered persecution. He was then sent to ʿAkka (or Acre) where after many hardships he died in 1892. His tomb has become a shrine revered by Baháʾís.

ʿAbduʾl-Bahá (1844–1921)

Baháʾuʾlláh was succeeded by his son, ʿAbduʾl-Bahá, known as ʿAbbas Effendi, who travelled widely in Europe and North America establishing Baháʾí religious communities. Baháʾí made its first Western converts in 1894 and continued to grow in the early years of the twentieth century. Many of the converts to Baháʾí came from groups that had strong mystical or occult leanings, or groups which were syncretistic and wanted to see a fusion of the better parts of different faith systems.

Greater organization

In 1921 the leadership of the movement was taken over by Baháʾuʾlláh's grandson, Shoghi Effendi Rabbani (1897–1957), who established a strong administrative system that ensured the expansion of Baháʾí. He regularized the faith and introduced important guidelines. He also set up many local and national organizations which could carry on the work of Baháʾí in the community. The missionary impetus of the movement was strong. When he died in 1957, he left a big gap and there was no clear guidance as to what should be done in terms of appointing a successor. In 1963 the Universal House of Justice was established as an administrative body to run Baháʾí.

In recent times adherence to the Baháʾí faith has continued to grow and membership may have passed 6 million. By far the greater amount of this growth has taken place in Latin America, Africa, and India. Iran is still an important centre for the Baháʾí faith, although believers

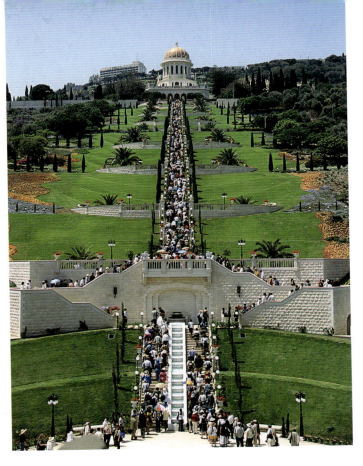

Delegates celebrate the inauguration of the terraces at the Shrine of the Báb, Haifa, Israel.

there have been socially excluded and persecuted, particularly since the 1979 revolution.

Branches of the Bahá'í Faith

The Bahá'í faith has generally maintained its unity, in that any sects which have arisen in opposition to the main branch of the faith have had little success in growth.

◆ Following the death of Bahá'u'lláh, authority passed to his son Abdu'l-Bahá, whose position was quickly questioned by his half-brother, Mirza Muhammad

The International Teaching Centre, Haifa, Israel.

'Ali. This led to a split in the movement and the creation of the Unitarian Bahá'ís. Apart from a few isolated adherents, this branch no longer exists.

◆ On his death in 1921 Abdu'l-Bahá appointed Shoghi Effendi Rabbani as his successor. Attempts were made to usurp his authority. This did not result in any significant splits, although followers in Germany, unhappy with the succession of Shoghi Effendi Rabbani, established a Free Bahá'í movement that has attracted a few hundred followers.

◆ Following the death of Shoghi Effendi Rabbani in 1957 there was an interregnum when leadership of the religion was assumed by a group of custodians. This resulted in further splits – with the creation of 'Bahá'ís under the Hereditary Guardianship' and the Orthodox Bahá'ís and 'Bahá'ís under the Provisions of the Covenant' – but none has had any significant impact.

Sacred Writings

Bahá'í scriptures, in the main, consist of the writings of Bahá'u'lláh and also the writings of his son, 'Abdu'l-Bahá. The Báb wrote over a six-year period, but much of his work is very difficult to read and to comprehend. As a result it is not widely known, although it does attract great respect.

The most important writings

Bahá'u'lláh continued to write extensively throughout his lifetime, even in those periods when he was imprisoned or in exile. His most important works include:

◆ the *Kitáb-i-Iqan* or 'Book of Certitude', which essentially deals with laws and instructions on how to live

◆ the *Kitáb-i-Aqdas* or 'Most Holy Book', which is more a treatise on theological questions. It is wide-ranging, providing a commentary on prophecies and teachings in the Bible and the Qur'an

◆ *Hidden Words* deals with spiritual and ethical issues

◆ *Seven Valleys* is a work of mystical quality.

Bahá'u'lláh's earlier works were mostly concerned with ethics and with mystical issues. His later writings show a much greater concern for introducing rules and guidelines, a sign that at this time he felt that the movement was consolidating and becoming more organized.

The authority of Bahá'í scriptures
The Báb's works are revered and both his and Bahá'u'lláh's writings carry the authority of sacred revelation, although Bahá'u'lláh did reject or alter some of the Báb's teachings.

'Abdu'l-Bahá's works are also scripture, but are regarded more as interpretation and commentary, in contrast to the revealed and inspired nature of the other two prophets. They do not carry the same authority as the writings of his grandfather.

Shoghi Effendi Rabbani wrote extensive commentaries on the writings of Bahá'u'lláh and 'Abdu'l-Bahá, but

these writings do not carry the status of scripture. They are, however, regarded as being infallible interpretations and are highly respected and honoured.

Core Beliefs

The Bahá'í faith emphasizes the unity of the entire human race. Religion should have as its primary purpose the promotion of harmony within humanity.

Bahá'í views of humanity
Religion is tasked with the creation of good order within human society. This good order will enable human progress and will empower human beings to attain their potential. The world itself is good and humans can attain to high moral ideals, although not all do. Bahá'í is very

An illuminated copy of the Kitáb-i-Aqdas, commissioned by 'Abdu'l-Bahá in 1902.

concerned with issues of justice, love and compassion. This optimistic view of humanity is strongly coupled with the belief that God is able to work through human beings to achieve his purpose in the world.

◆ The founders of the world religions were prophets, sent by the one God, to guide humanity and to release the divine power in each human being.

◆ The Báb and Bahá'u'lláh are manifestations of the divine in their own age, in the same way that other prophets were for theirs.

◆ The revelation given by God through each of the prophets shows evidence of

progression, and so the development of world religions is also the story of the interaction between humanity and God over millennia.

◆ Each prophet has taught an aspect of the whole truth.

◆ In this age, the unity of humanity is even more important and Bahá'í seeks to promote world government, inter-faith discussion, and racial harmony.

◆ Bahá'í is strongly pacifist.

◆ It believes that all are equal.

All of human existence, then, is the story of individual and corporate progress towards the divine. This progress is aided by the prophets who are born at various times in history and who show the way forward. Each one, through his or her teaching, brings about a greater degree of social development for the whole of humanity. Education plays a very important role in enabling humanity to be self-reflective.

The Lotus Temple in New Delhi, India.

Worship and Festivals

Bahá'í worship consists of few formal rituals. In essence, worship borrows extensively from Bahá'í's Islamic roots.

Prayer and pilgrimage

Bahá'ís use many prayers composed by both Bahá'u'lláh and 'Abdu'l-Bahá in their prayer times. *Salat* is the term given to private prayer, which is directed towards the tomb of Bahá'u'lláh at 'Akka. It is performed three times a day. The final month of the Bahá'í year – Bahá'í follow the solar calendar – is one of fasting.

Pilgrimage is valued. Shiraz in Iran is a holy city to Bahá'ís, being the place where the Báb revealed his divine mission in 1844. Worshippers also travel to the Haifa-'Akka area to visit the holy shrines of Bahá'u'lláh, 'Abdu'l-Bahá and the Báb.

Meeting for worship

Bahá'í has no priesthood. Meetings and gatherings are organized by local assemblies. These gatherings are generally informal and lack ritual. The main gatherings are held every nineteen days. The Nineteen-day Feast is held on the first day of the Bahá'í month. There are also nine holy days each year to celebrate important events in the lives of the Báb and Bahá'u'llah. These days are meant to be free of work and are usually held in the homes of believers. Here, prayers are recited and the holy scriptures are read. They are also times for special meals and fellowship.

Bahá'ís do not, in general, have special buildings for worship. They meet either in rented buildings or in homes. There are only a few formal worship buildings in use worldwide, currently seven temples on different continents.

Rites of passage

When a child is born into the Bahá'í faith, he or she is named in a special, but simple, ceremony. Marriage ceremonies are also simple. They involve a minimum of ritual, with some scriptures being read and music being used in accordance with the culture in which the ceremony takes place. Funerals are required to follow certain prescribed rules. The burial (cremation is frowned upon) should take place no more than one hour's distance from where the person has died. At burial, the feet of the deceased must face in the direction of the tomb of Bahá'u'lláh.

Family and Society

The family is the most important social unit. Marriage is strongly encouraged and the proper raising of children in a stable home environment is promoted vigorously. Divorce is permitted in the case of the total breakdown of a relationship, but it is expected that the couple will use all means possible to avoid the breakup of the family unit.

Bahá'ís in wider society

Because of the nature of Bahá'í, it seeks to influence society as a whole. Its goal is to create a more harmonious and spiritually aware society, where human beings are progressing in knowledge of the divine and

Bahá'ís at a prayer meeting in Memphis, USA.

where this is manifested in increased social justice, love, and compassion. Bahá'ís are encouraged to think of themselves as part of a much wider community. They are not merely individuals, but have social responsibilities. The role of women in society is strongly respected and equality of the sexes is a fundamental part of the Bahá'í world-view.

Bahá'ís are very involved at all levels of society and the faith encourages good government with high standards. It is believed that where government seeks the best for the people and where it lives up to high standards, then the nation will prosper in every way and individuals will benefit and be part of a just society. Social teaching and social justice are key foundations of the Bahá'í faith.

Contemporary Issues

Bahá'í is well placed for growth and expansion in the contemporary world since its fundamental ideals are very much at one with the trend towards harmony of faith and human solidarity in tackling political, environmental, and social problems. As various groupings strive for recognition and equality, the fact that the Bahá'í faith focuses on such ideals means that it can give good examples and a wealth of advice born of much experience.

Bahá'ís have been involved in a myriad of social projects throughout the world and the faith's work with both UNESCO and UNICEF has been praised. It raises considerable amounts of money for social projects, particularly those which focus on the elimination of poverty and the promotion of equality and social inclusion.

Bahá'í life ceremonies

Bahá'ís are encouraged to marry and believe that the main purpose of the marriage bond is to bring about procreation. In Bahá'í marriage, the husband and wife are regarded as being not only physically but also spiritually united and therefore will enjoy eternal unity. Physical attraction alone will not bring about stability in the marriage and will make the marriage bond insecure. The consent of all four living parents of both parties must be obtained before any marriage can go ahead. Parents cannot, however, choose a spouse for their child and all parties to a marriage must give full consent. Bahá'ís are allowed to marry non-Bahá'ís and can be married in non-Bahá'í ceremonies, but the Bahá'í party should also have a Bahá'í ceremony either before or after the ceremony of the partner of the other faith.

Divorce is allowed under strictly exceptional circumstances, but it is severely frowned upon. Advice on the state of the marriage is sought and the Bahá'í Spiritual Assembly will try to resolve difficulties.

Bahá'ís do not agree with cremation. Burial is the norm amongst them. It is considered that since the human body is formed in a gradual way over a long period of time, so it should be allowed to decompose in a similar timeframe.[2]

Reading guide to the Bahá'í faith

Cardin, Heather, ed., *A Warm Place in My Heart: Young Voices on Faith*, George Ronald, Oxford, 2007.

Miller, William McElwhee, *What is the Bahá'í Faith?*, William Eerdmans, Grand Rapids, Michigan, 1977.

Momen, Moojan, ed., *Studies in Bábi and Bahá'í History*, Vol. I, Kalimat Press, Los Angeles, 1982.

Sinclair, Guy, *A Study Guide to the Constitution of the Universal House of Justice*, George Ronald, Oxford, 2005.

Smith, Peter, *The Bábi and Bahá'í Religions: From Messianic Shi'ism to a World Religion*, Cambridge University Press, 1987.

The development of Bahá'í as a very recent religion is interesting. Although it has its roots in Islam, it has been considerably influenced by Western ideas and methods and in its short history it has developed a surprisingly distinct identity. The movement is, however, prone to authoritarianism in its attempts to maintain this strong identity and this may lead in time to a degree of fragmentation.

Inside the Haifa Bahá'í Cemetery, Haifa, Israel.

Hinduism

History and Development

The origins of Hinduism pre-date written texts. Hindus often speak of it as the oldest living religion, the *sanatana dharma* or 'eternal' religion. Despite its ancient roots it is difficult to identify, because there is such wide variation of opinion within Hinduism about almost all aspects of the religion.

Size With up to a billion members worldwide, Hinduism is generally considered to be the third largest religion in the world.

Founder No single founder; many teachers and schools of thought.

Location Originating in the Indian sub-continent by about 2500 BCE, probably in the Indus valley, Hinduism has in recent times established communities abroad, including about a million Hindus in the US and up to a million in the UK.

Since the nineteenth century the term 'Hinduism' has been used widely in the West to describe the belief systems of the majority of India's population. Hindus tend not to describe themselves as such, in general identifying themselves in terms of their caste or community or adherence to a particular deity. Hinduism is:

◆ the faith of 800–900 million people in India, the majority of Nepal's population of 23 million, and smaller numbers in many other countries;

◆ a diverse set of beliefs and traditions grouped into a single system – not only a religious system, but a culture that influences social and political life;

◆ a polytheistic faith, in that its adherents worship many gods and goddesses, but many Hindus believe these deities are manifestations of one supreme power;

◆ a religion without a single founder or a unified set of doctrines;

◆ a philosophic experience, using meditation or other means to explore the relationship between the human soul or *atman* and that which is divine;

◆ a religion with a canon of ancient texts, the Vedas, sacred to many people, but to which others do not ascribe the same importance or authority;

◆ a religion that can accommodate areas that are not theistic as well as significant strands that believe in a creator God.

In general, Hindus believe in a God who is transcendent; that is, outside of the created order and above it. This belief is balanced, as in other religious traditions, with the notion that God is also immanent; that is, present and operative in the world and even in human beings.

Within India

The beginnings of Hinduism appear to lie in the Indus valley. It has been held that around 2,500 BCE a tribe of Indo-European descent, the Aryans, supplanted a civilization that had grown up in the Indus valley, bringing with them their language, Sanskrit, and their religious traditions. Many scholars challenge this view. To some, recent archaeological discoveries indicate that the religion emerged earlier from within India.

A central feature of Hinduism is the caste system, which influences all aspects of an individual's life, particularly with regard to career and personal choices. Because of the caste system, society is hierarchical. The basis for the system is the doctrine of *karma*, by which actions in one life determine the outcome of the next. Status in the next existence depends on right or wrong actions in the previous one.

Around the sixth century BCE pressure for reform within Hinduism found expression in the creation of two new religions, Buddhism and Jainism.

Outside India

Hinduism has exercised influence worldwide through the Hindu diaspora (those Hindus who migrated to different

The sacred Hindu sign Om, in a temple in India. 'Om' is the sound associated with the Absolute, the source of all existence. When 'Om' is spoken or chanted, it is believed to contain great power, containing within it the essence of all truth.

parts of the globe). As Hindus have settled in new areas they have carried with them their customs and beliefs, successfully planting Hindu philosophy or aspects of it in many non-Indian contexts, particularly in the West. India, as it has increased in wealth and importance through industrialization, has become a major player in world markets and many Indians have travelled abroad to study and work. Today significant Hindu communities exist in the US, Australia, Britain, and continental Europe. The former kingdom of Nepal, a republic since 2008, remains a strongly Hindu nation.

Founder and Significant Figures

A consequence of Hinduism's ancient origins and broad composition and belief base is that there is no single founding figure within it and no single authoritative text that pronounces on doctrine. Teaching is contained within a corpus or collection of ancient holy books and over the centuries numerous influential philosophical schools have grown up, each embracing a different world-view and interpretation of theology.

Religious teachers

Hindu myth refers to a group of seven wise men known as *rishis*. These men passed on the wisdom of the gods to humankind. Their task finished, they were transformed into the constellation Ursa Major. From there each *rishi* may still guide human beings, especially those on physical or metaphysical journeys.

The earthly successors to the *rishis* are thought to be Hindu priests of the Brahmin caste, who have an important role in day-to-day Hindu religious practice.

Another type of guide or teacher, the *guru*, has a role in teaching about faith and enlightenment. Gurus have a different role from priests (although some gurus are Brahmins). They do not generally engage in ritual, but are thinkers and philosophers who are sought out by disciples for their wisdom. Similarly, a *swami* is a holy man who may be listened to for his knowledge.

Branches of Hinduism

Branches of the Hindu faith tend to take the form of philosophical schools of thought or indeed sub-schools. They may differ, for example, over the question of dualism or non-dualism, *dvaida* or *advaida*, when seeking to characterize the relationship between the ultimate reality and the human soul or *atman*.

The school commanding the largest following today, *Vedanta*, owes much to the philosopher-saint Shankara, who was born in the eighth century CE in southern India and placed a high value on the Hindu sacred texts known as the Vedas. Patanjali by contrast, who lived about six centuries earlier, was an authoritative figure within the yoga schools of thought. His interpretations of yogic philosophy are considered to represent the classical form of the practice.

Vedanta

Shankara's non-dualistic teachings focus

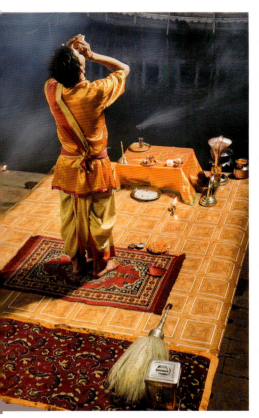

◆ This illusion holds the blinded *atman* in a continuous cycle of life and death.

◆ Liberation for human beings is achieved when they escape *maya* by recognizing their oneness with Brahman.

◆ Liberation means release from the cycle of life and death.

◆ Many Hindu teachers believe that the world only appears to be real, although there is much disagreement on the concept of *maya*. Other philosophers of the *Vedanta* school have built on Shankara's ideas while disagreeing with key elements of what he taught.

◆ Ramanuja (traditionally 1017–1137 CE) rejected the concept of *maya*.

◆ Madhva (c. 1199–1278 CE) promoted a *dvaida* version of *Vedanta*, denying the union between Brahman and *atman*.

◆ Gadadhar Chattopadhyay (1836–76 CE), who later took the name Ramakrishna, founded the Ramakrishna movement, teaching that all religions are true and that serving humanity is the most effective worship of God.

◆ Ramakrishna's pupil Swami Vivekananda (1863–1902) is credited with bringing Hinduism to the West and raising inter-faith awareness. He founded numerous Vedanta societies.

Yogic philosophy

The Hindu-related term 'yoga' carries in its root the sense of 'uniting' or 'joining'. The goal of this discipline is to experience

A Brahmin performing the Ganga Aarti ceremony.

on reality. The only reality, he argues, is Brahman, to be understood as ultimate reality and absolute, pure consciousness. The human soul or *atman* is identified with this absolute reality, but is unaware of this unity, being blinded by an illusion, or *maya*.

◆ According to Shankara, *maya* is the powerful illusion that the world is real.

unity with that which is highest. It brings about the transformation of consciousness. The school of yoga most familiar in the West is *Hatha Yoga*, largely made up of breathing and postural exercises. However, yoga encompasses far more than bodily exercise. In achieving the transformation of consciousness it draws on the *Samkhya* philosophical school. In this influential school of thought, reality is made up of *purusa*, which can be understood as consciousness, and *prakrti*, which refers to the natural or the material.

The most renowned teacher of the yoga path is Patanjali, author of the *Yoga-Sutra*. Its basis probably dates from the second century CE and may have been drafted some centuries earlier. Yoga did not originate with Patanjali, but he is an influential commentator. To him the essence of yoga is the cessation of the whirlwind of thought. It is about achieving a unified consciousness which in turn manifests an awareness of the unity of all things. This is done through the quieting of thought. His *Yoga-Sutra* consists of almost 200 *sutras* which explain how this can be achieved.

Patanjali's philosophy proposes that people can attain almost supernatural powers of spiritual perception through yoga. He enumerated eight areas of yogic practice which are known as the 'eight limbs' or *astanga* of yoga.

Brahmo Samaj

There is debate as to how far reform movements can be viewed as expressions of Hinduism if they seek to redefine too

A yogi plays the flute at sunrise near the Ganges river in India.

many key features of the religion. Founded by Ram Mohan Roy (1772–1833), the Brahmo Samaj was influenced by Christian ideas. Roy was familiar with the Christian scriptures and with the Unitarian movement. His writings on Jesus show that he viewed Jesus not as a divine being, but as a moral and ethical man who exercised compassion. Critical of many Hindu practices, Roy highlighted the importance of rationalism and humanism as tools to reform Hinduism.

Unitarian Christians emphasize Jesus' humanity and his role as an ethical and moral reformer of society; they do not stress or hold a trinitarian concept of God. Roy looked to Hindu scriptural texts, the *Dharma Shastras* and *Upanishads*, and found many resonances and parallels with the Christianity expressed in Unitarianism. He wanted to foster a Hindu spirituality, but wished to reject *sati*, the burning of widows on the funeral pyres of their husbands, and other practices which he considered to be inhumane and irrational and not in accordance with true classical Hinduism. Roy also rejected polytheism, reincarnation, and scriptures that he felt stood in the way of progress and development, particularly in the field of social reform.

In his attempts to blend aspects of Christianity with Hinduism, Roy alienated himself to some degree from both paths. Christians could not accept his unorthodox version of Christianity. Hindus felt he had abandoned core principles of Hinduism to promote Christianity in their stead.

Astanga Yoga – The eightfold practice

Yama   Practices to be avoided so that liberation can be achieved.

Niyama   Qualities and practices to be nurtured.

Asana   Achieving a relaxed posture.

Pranayama   Correct use of *prana* or the energy which is all around human beings; since *prana* is in the air, breathing meaningfully can increase our energy.

Pratyahara   Detachment from the world around us, allowing us to focus on the more important goal, and concentrate.

Dharana   Concentration brought about by *pratyahara*.

Dhyana   Meditation that follows from sustained concentration.

Samadhi   Deep contemplation, which can be a state of trance.

Arya Samaj

Founded by Dayananda Sarasvati (1824–83), the Arya Samaj highlighted the importance of the Vedas and sought a purer Hinduism, free of the corruption he felt had crept into the faith in the post-Vedic era. Whereas Roy had preached the importance of the *Upanishads*, Sarasvati held to the divine revelation as expressed in the earliest Vedic texts, in the *Rig-Veda* in particular.

◆ Sarasvati wanted Hindus to return to a form of religious practice in which child marriage and widow-burning or *sati* were unknown.

◆ He strongly rejected Christianity and regarded the Vedas as superior to Muslim or Sikh scriptures.

◆ He wanted Hindus to be proud of their heritage and referred them back to the ancient Aryan civilization, hoping that identification with this noble society would help Hindus of his day to regain their sense of morality and importance.

In the West

Aside from reform movements and new expressions of traditional Hinduism, modern times have seen a considerable Hindu influence on a variety of new religious or meditative movements in the West, some attracting media attention through a striking lifestyle or interest shown by the Beatles or film stars such as Clint Eastwood.

Among the Indians to find a Western following may be included: Dada Lekhraj (1876–1969) who founded the Brahma Kumaris or 'daughters of Brahma'; Swami A. C. Bhaktivedanta Praphupada (1896–1977) who founded the Hare Krishna movement (officially ISKCON); the Maharishi Mahesh Yogi (1918–2008) who established Transcendental Meditation (TM); and the 'boy guru' of the Divine Light Mission, Prem Rawat (b. 1958), whose initial teaching may have derived in part from the Sant tradition of northern India.

Nationalism

In the twenty-first century India has experienced a revival of Hindu nationalism, with the establishment of political parties that seek to bring Hindu cultural and religious values to the forefront of the country's policy and practice.

Sacred Writings

Hindu sacred writings can be categorized as either revealed to ancient sages directly from God, *sruti*, or remembered and written down from memory by humans, *smrti*. *Sruti* scriptures enjoy a higher status than *smrti* texts.

The Vedic canon

The term 'veda' stands for 'knowledge' and the collections of texts that are held most sacred within Hinduism are called 'the Veda' or 'the Vedas'. At the heart of this canon are four collections that represent an early stage of Hinduism. Written in an early form of Sanskrit (meaning 'refined') they consist of a body of texts compiled over many centuries and regarded as revealed scriptures, perfect compositions with a divine origin. It is difficult to date these texts, with time spans proposed for individual pieces within a period of 1500–200 BCE. Brahmin scholars, traditionally held to belong to the highest class within society, have a particular role in interpreting the Vedic collections, which comprise four principal types:

◆ The Vedic *Samhitas* are known as the *Rig-Veda* (also written *Rg-Veda*), the *Sama-Veda*, the *Yajur-Veda* and the *Atharva-Veda*. They include hymns of praise to a variety of gods, showing early attempts to understand nature and the deities behind natural forces, as well as *mantras* or sacred sentences to be chanted.

◆ The *Brahmanas* explain rituals, especially those connected with Agni, the fire god.

◆ The *Aranyakas* deal strongly with philosophical and contemplative themes.

◆ The *Upanishads* are commentaries on the core texts, concentrating on the spiritual development of the individual human. Scholars judge that they were composed between 600 and 300 BCE.

A Thai traditional dance, featuring Rama, monkey Hanuman, and Totsagan, king of the devils.

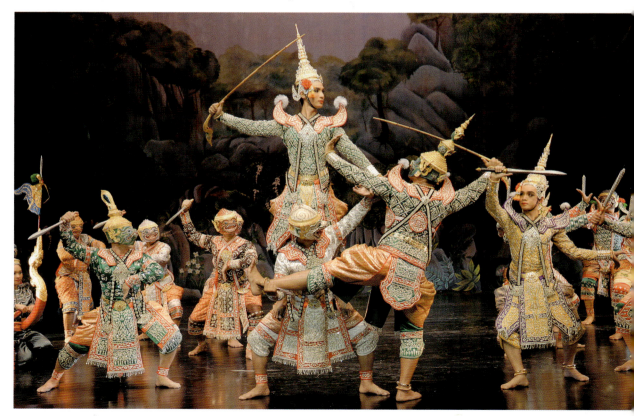

In this 16th-century illustration, a battle between Babhruvahana and the snakes is depicted. Babhruvahana, the son of Arjuna the archer in Hinduism, fights against the snakes of the nether regions. Peacocks and other birds attack the snakes, some of which are hooded cobras. The men stand in chariots or ride horses with decorated coverings, and some use bows and arrows. It is taken from the Persian version of the Mahabharata, Parvans XIV–XVIII. The authorship of the poem is traditionally ascribed to the sage Vyasa, although it is more likely that he compiled existing material.

The Upanishads

In the *Upanishads* the idea of the human soul or *atman* is very significant. It is understood not as separate from Brahman, the absolute being in the universe, but as the very essence of Brahman, living in the individual. This unity between *atman* and the Brahman is achieved through self-sacrifice. However, sacrifice is not understood, as it is in the earliest Vedic texts, in terms of offering up meat and vegetables, but rather as internal sacrifice and spiritual transformation. The unity of *atman* and Brahman brings to the human being a higher form of both wisdom and knowledge.

Ramayana, Mahabharata, Bhagavad Gita

Sacred writings classified as *smrti* do not have the same divine authority as the Vedas, but nevertheless teach important spiritual truths and enjoy considerable influence amongst Hindus. Epic tales of good and evil such as the *Ramayana* and the *Mahabharata* are extremely popular and are told and retold in story, song and dance. Both texts were finalized around 400 CE, but their content is considerably older. Each is an important cultural repository. By expressing ancient wisdom and philosophy in narrative form they had a profound effect on later Indian culture.

◆ The *Ramayana* tells the story of the young prince Rama and his wife, Sita. The story is thought to be about 2,500 years old. It explores the themes of good and evil and the role of the gods in human affairs. Like the *Mahabharata*, the *Ramayana* is an important cultural repository. It has had a profound effect on later Indian culture and it expresses ancient wisdom and philosophy in narrative form.

◆ The *Mahabharata* also deals with the confrontation between good and evil through exploring the relationships between two rival family factions. It ushers in the age of Kali, an age in which noble human ideals are severely compromised by the influence of evil and immorality.

◆ The *Mahabharata* contains certain teachings from Krishna, an incarnation or avatar of the god Vishnu. Whilst an integral part of the *Mahabharata*, these teachings form the *Bhagavad Gita*, which has developed as a popular text.

◆ The *Bhagavad Gita* or 'Song of God' is a conversation between Krishna and Arjuna, a principal character and hero of the *Mahabharata* epic, on the eve of a major battle between good and evil, the battle of Kurukshetra. In this conversation Krishna teaches Hindu philosophy in clear and concise terms and this is part of the reason for the popularity of the *Gita*.

The Puranas

The *Puranas* are collections of writings that tell the stories of kings, gods, wise men, and heroes. There are eighteen major *Puranas* and eighteen minor ones. The term *purana* means 'ancient' and many of the stories are about the distant past. They were collected

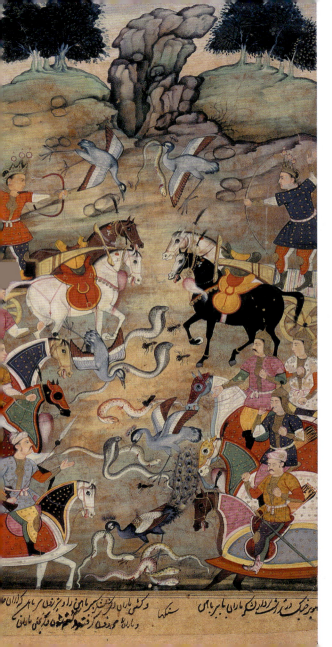

and written some time between 500 and 1500 CE, although some scholars place their completion as early as 1000 CE and the beginning of their composition as far back as 300 BCE. The tales stress 'devotion' or *bhakti* and deal with the idea of pilgrimage and the relevance of holy places and sites of worship. They also highlight genealogies and legal matters.

Core Beliefs

As a result of its diversity and the lack of a centralized authority, Hindu religious doctrine and practice varies, although there are certain common strands throughout most expressions of the faith. It is also important to realize that Hinduism is embedded within culture.

Deities

Hindus honour a great number of gods and goddesses, although some Hindus may be monotheistic, believing that the myriad of deities worshipped are simply expressions of one single, supreme, divine figure. This god may have many names. However, they believe that he is Brahman, the one behind the many other manifestations. In modern times the two gods most worshipped by Hindus are Vishnu and Shiva.

Karma, samsara and dharma

Hindus believe that actions determine future lives. There is, therefore, a moral basis or reason for each person's status in this life, since it has been earned by actions in the previous one. The doctrine is intimately linked with the concepts of *samsara* and *dharma*.

The god Shiva

Shiva is understood in terms of contradictions, polarities or extremes. He can be kind, yet menacing. He is a creator, but also the destroyer. He may be joyful, or stern and austere. He is associated with both life and death. It is also usual to link Shiva with sexuality and he is worshipped in the phallic form. The consort of Shiva is Parvati. She is kind and gentle. Another of his consorts, Kali, is less reassuring, but Hindus believe that her appearance – holding a sword, wearing a necklace of skulls and dripping blood from her mouth – means she can frighten off and subdue evil. Shiva and Parvati's son Ganesha, the elephant-headed god, is the lifter of burdens, the one who clears the road of life. Devotion to Shiva is known as *Shaivism*.

The god Vishnu

As taught in the Vedas, Vishnu was originally the god of the sky. He shows himself in the world of humans in many forms, particularly in times of darkness and need. These manifestations can be called 'incarnations' or avatars. One such avatar is Krishna, a major figure in the *Bhagavad Gita*. Rama is another incarnation of Vishnu. In all, Vishnu has ten incarnations, nine of which have taken place; the final incarnation is yet to come. However, various lists of the incarnations exist and differ from each other.

Those who worship Vishnu are known as *Vaishnava* or 'worshippers of Vishnu'. The worship of Vishnu is a thriving expression of Hindu faith today and many of the most popular temples and sites of worship are dedicated to him. Vishnu is thought to fight against evil and is strongly linked to the promotion of the law and of righteousness or *dharma*. In many of his incarnations, Vishnu is joined by his consort, Lakshmi or Sri. She is worshipped as a goddess in her own right.

- *Samsara* is the belief that humans are destined to be continuously reborn in a cycle of reincarnation until they achieve *moksha*, which is liberation or freedom from the cycle. The store of one's actions is built up over several lifetimes.

- The term *karma* literally means 'action', but it carries the sense of reward and punishment for those actions. The results of *karma* may last for several lifetimes. *Karma* has consequences not only for the spiritual status of the individual, but also for social status. Bad actions will lead to the soul being reborn in lower levels of society or even as part of the animal world.

- Liberation from *samsara* comes about

Sculpture of a dancing Shiva at Shiva Temple, Gangaikonda Cholapuram, India.

as a result of right living. This right living leads to enlightenment and higher wisdom, which enable the human being to experience the transformation which brings about *moksha*.

The *Upanishads* are important as sources of teaching about *karma*. They make a distinction between 'lower' and 'higher' wisdom. Part of practising right action is to fulfil one's obligations according to what is expected. The duty an individual is expected to meet or fulfil is known as *dharma* or 'the law', which is associated with the whole order of the universe, the whole of the moral order, social order, and personal righteousness.

A 1653 illustration for the seventh book of the *Ramayana*, an ancient Sanskrit epic attributed to the poet Valmiki. In the bottom half, the gods ask Shiva and Parvati for help against the Rakshasas (demons). The gods who were sent to Vishnu by Shiva repeat their request which is granted in the top half.

Avatars

Avataras or avatars are incarnations of gods. The word originally means 'down-coming' or 'descent'. It is especially applied to the descents to the world of humans by the god Vishnu, although it can be applied to manifestations of other gods. The *Bhagavad Gita* teaches that, when the truth is in danger, avatars come to the earth to guide people to the true path again.

The avatars of Vishnu

The avatars of Vishnu are generally numbered as ten. The *dasavataras* (ten descents) include animal forms as well as the human forms of Rama and Krishna. The most common ten descents are listed as:
Matsya, the fish
Hamsa, the swan
Kurma, the tortoise
Varaha, the boar
Nrsinha, the man-lion
Varmana, the dwarf
Rama, with the axe (also known as Parashurama)
Rama
Krishna
Kalkin
Krishna is regarded as the greatest human incarnation of Vishnu. Kalkin or Kalki is an avatar which is yet to be manifest and will be revealed at the end of time.

The four goals

Hindu teaching sets out four goals which human beings can aspire to achieve. There is no order of priority to the goals. All four are regarded as acceptable.

◆ The goal of attaining material things, wealth, and power is called *artha*.

◆ The goal of personal gratification and happiness, meaning sensual pleasure, including sexual pleasure and the love of beauty, is called *kama*.

◆ *Dharma* is the performance of duty and the practice of good religious behaviour, which will eventually lead to liberation or *moksha*.

◆ *Moksha* is the fourth goal, and is liberation from the cycle of *samsara*.

Paths to a deeper union

The *Bhagavad Gita* teaches that there are three paths that enable the soul to escape the cycle of birth and rebirth and finally achieve unity with the Absolute, which is the source of the soul and of all creation.

◆ The first is the path of knowledge, known as *jnanayoga*. However, the path of *jnana* is concerned not simply with the knowledge that comes from books (although it is important to learn from the scriptures). *Jnana* means having knowledge and understanding of Brahman, enabling the soul to identify itself not with the world, but with the universal soul, which is Brahman.

◆ The path of action, *karmayoga*, is the second. It focuses the Hindu believer on the performance of duty and the dedication of one's actions to God. The performance of work from a selfless perspective can lead to release and fulfilment. The path of karma also includes performing rituals in daily life. As with *jnana*, the path of *karma* leads the individual to being conscious of the fact that he or she is an eternal being with an eternal dimension.

◆ *Bhaktiyoga*, the third path, is the way of devotion. It is identified with a selfless love of God. The believer directs trust and love towards God and seeks to enjoy his presence. God, in turn, helps the soul towards liberation. Many of the heroes of the *Puranas* are held up as examples of *bhakti*, because of the ways in which they serve each other or are devoted in love to

The four stages of life

Hinduism views life as divided into four stages. Each reflects the spiritual development in the life of the individual as he or she pursues the four goals of life: *dharma*, the practice of righteous living; *artha*, the pursuit of material well-being; *kama*, the sensual pleasures of life; and *moksha*, final liberation.

The student stage, *brahmacharya*, begins at around the age of 8 to 12, when a child attains a moral awareness and thus moral responsibility. Initiation may be involved. In some families children are instructed by a guru.

The householder phase begins when the student gets married and needs to build a home and gather wealth. Becoming a householder or *grhastya* also entails righteous living or *dharma*, since the person is expected to behave in a responsible way towards society and towards the wider family.

In the stage of the forest-dweller or *vnaprasthya,* a married couple will be less engaged with the pursuit of worldly wealth and sensual pleasure; they will withdraw from society to engage in more spiritual activities.

The fourth stage of life is *samnyasa*, the period of renunciation of worldly goods and pleasures and a time when all the individual's attention should be focused on attaining complete liberation or *moksha*.

The third and fourth stages are not followed by all Hindus, but a significant number of people do renounce the world to wander from place to place living a spiritual existence. Male renouncers are known as *samnyasis* and women as *samnyasinis*.[1]

each other. Hindu devotees may choose their own particular deity (*ista deva*) to whom they may offer *bhakti*.

Worship and Festivals

Hindu worship demonstrates the diversity of Hindu religious belief. Religious ritual and ritualistic devotions to deities can take place anywhere. Religious devotion can be shown in temples that have been dedicated to a particular deity, at home before images

Opposite: Frangipani flowering in the garden of a Hindu temple, Bali, Indonesia.

of the gods, or in special places that are considered holy and to which groups of people may travel in pilgrimage. Hindus can worship both as individuals and as part of a corporate group.

Temple or home

The Hindu offering of worship is known as *puja*. A temple will have within it an image of the particular deity to whom it is dedicated and to whom *puja* is directed. Every temple will have its own priests. A temple priest is known as a *pujari*. Many of the priests will be Brahmins and will belong to the priestly class. They carry out the rituals within the temple.

The worship of the god or goddess may involve the image of the deity being ritually cleansed and even offered food. Many Hindu homes will have a special room – it may be a hallway – where the image of the god or goddess worshipped is displayed. This is known as a *puja* room. Depending on how devout the householder is, worship will be offered at various points in the day. Sometimes a householder might invite a priest to the home to perform a ritual.

Temples may be large, ornate buildings or simple village structures. Even when taking part in *puja* as a group, worshippers see themselves as offering individual rather than congregational worship. In large temples ceremonies may take place throughout the day. At sunrise the god will be wakened, dressed, and fed. Worshippers will then offer a constant stream of prayers, sometimes garlanding the image in

A Balinese Hindu cremation procession.

flowers and incense. In the evening the god will be put to rest. Worshippers will also give offerings of food and money to the priests to assist in the running of the temple.

Goddess worship

Shakti, which means 'power or strength', is used in Hindu belief to describe the creative power a goddess manifests, or divine female power. The goddess tradition is very influential in Hindu culture. Many goddesses are worshipped and a goddess is often seen in ambivalent terms. She can be kind and gentle, the source of life; she can also be demanding or vengeful. Almost all Hindus will have some adherence to a goddess tradition. Those who have a particular devotion to goddess worship are known as *shaktas*. Within *Vaishnavism* and *Shaivism*, devotion to *shakti* is often expressed through the veneration of the consorts of male gods. *Shakti* is also used to describe the power in all divine figures.

Sacred cows

The cow is an important figure of worship in India. Cows are seen as sacred creatures, even as the incarnation of the goddess Devi. Cow dung is often used in *puja*. Killing the cow is strongly against the principles of Hinduism.

Life-cycle rituals

Significant milestones are commemorated in life-cycle rituals, known collectively as *samskaras*. There are over forty possible *samskara* rituals ranging from the pre-natal to those after death. Pregnant women are

given charms to protect them in childbirth, and the birth of a child is celebrated, followed by a cleansing ritual. The ceremony of *namkaran* is a naming ritual, and detailed astrological charts may be kept to be consulted when key decisions have to be made either for or by the child. For many girls the first menstruation is acknowledged as an important event. Boys from the higher castes go through a ceremony when they pass from childhood to adulthood; they are given a sacred thread and are taught certain scriptures. If a marriage is arranged – nowadays a less common practice – astrological charts will be consulted to

A Balinese Hindu woman looks back at the procession.

Pilgrims in colourful attire at the ghats in Varanasi. They flock to the Ganges river to perform puja, a religious ritual. They bring offerings to Mother Ganges and believe that the holy water cleanses them from all sins.

confirm the suitability of a potential match. The ceremonies performed at death are known as *shraddha*. It is important to perform them correctly to aid the rebirth. Hindus cremate their dead at a cremation site known as a *ghat*.

Pilgrimage

This is an important part of Hindu worship. Numerous sites are considered sacred, including rivers, mountains, springs, and even whole cities, such as Allahabad. The waters of the River Ganges are regarded as especially holy. On pilgrimage, Hindus will perform special rituals and give offerings. It is believed that pilgrimage brings healing and spiritual transformation. The Kumbha Mela, which takes place every three years in northern India, attracts millions of people.

Festivals

Some festivals last just a day, others spread over several days. Each important deity will have a special day and processions will honour the god or goddess. The most important festivals are very bright and colourful. They usually consist of dance performances and acts of storytelling as well as songs and music. These cultural expressions of devotion will tell stories about the deities and about their relationships to human beings. Many Hindus carry a pocket almanac, a diary that organizes the year according to the Western, solar or lunar calendars.

Diwali

Around the autumnal equinox Hindu families throughout the world will set up lights to 'guide' Lakshmi, the goddess of wealth, and give gifts to each other.

Sri Panchami

This winter festival, dedicated to Saraswati, goddess of learning, is celebrated by students. Young children are encouraged to practise their early writing skills.

Shivaratri

Around January–February Shiva is celebrated. The followers of the god will fast and give offerings.

Holi

This spring festival honours Krishna as a playful or 'trickster' god. To follow his example people sing in the street and engage in all kinds of pranks. Tricks may be played on authority figures. Traditional roles may be

turned on their heads. People throw water and coloured powder at each other.

Dashara

In the autumn, usually just before the rice harvest, Dashara or Dussehra celebrates the birth of Rama and his defeat of the demon-king Ravana. Particularly in Bengal it is twinned with a celebration of Durga and her defeat of demon forces.

Family and Society

Many Hindu family units are extended ones. These can also be known as 'joint families'. In Hindu society several generations of one family may live together under the same roof. The family, even in modern times when members may live at some distance from each other, is still regarded as a very important unit within society and parents can continue to have strong influence on their children. Traditionally, Hindu family structures are male dominated, as is Hindu society as a whole. However, women are increasingly well educated and are often involved in high level employment, particularly in urban areas.

The banks of the River Ganges are lit up with thousands of candles for the Festival of Lights.

Caste

In Hinduism social structure is very distinct because of the caste system. This system plays a major role in regulating society. It is a stratified system. This means that some groups are considered of higher importance and social standing than others. The word 'caste' is of Portuguese origin and means 'pure'. Caste involves a complicated hierarchy of groups, which are almost like large families. They have even been described as having the character of large trade unions, since members of a particular caste will traditionally have followed a certain occupation. Good *karma* in the past is believed to lead to one being born into a higher caste. Generally, Hindus marry and socialize within their own castes, but in modern times the interaction between castes is much more flexible than in the past. However, intermarriage between people from the higher castes and the dalits, who are regarded as belonging to the lowest caste, or even of such lowly status to be outside of the caste system, would still be rare and frowned upon, as would intermarriage between those of higher caste and other lower caste members.

Contemporary Issues

In India, where most Hindus live, society has undergone many changes in recent times. Some of these have helped Hinduism to spread its teachings to a wider audience. Television transmits elaborate and lavish presentations of the great Hindu epics and these are very popular. Hinduism

The caste system

Perhaps one of the most distinctive aspects of Hinduism is the caste system.[2] This is a social system with a very strict hierarchical structure. Each caste incorporates a certain traditional occupation or function within society. Hindus believe that the system has a divine origin. It does certainly have its roots in ancient Vedic religion, where the ideal social system was believed to consist of four *varnas* or social groupings. Each of these groups was involved in a specific occupation.

- *Brahmins* made up the priestly and scholarly class.
- *Kshatriyas* were the warriors and the rulers of society, regarded as a noble class.
- *Vaishyas* engaged in commercial ventures and business activities.
- *Shudras* were those whose function it was to serve the other three groups.

It is believed that one is born into a lower or higher caste as the result of one's actions in previous lives, a result of *karma*.

has become much better known outside India and Nepal and it attracts many people worldwide to its teachings. Yoga and other spiritual disciplines which originate in Hinduism are practised by people from all walks of life all over the world.

Within India itself the middle classes are looking to exponents of Hindu reform movements and breakaway shoots and sects who preach a form of the faith which they can integrate into their modern, busy, and urban lives. Some of these may emphasize a more liberationist approach for women. Many of the new teachers of Hinduism have devoted followers outside of India and traditional Hindu religious structures.

As in many other faiths, Hinduism has to face the threat of secularism and this has given rise to fundamentalist tendencies in certain quarters.

Hindu fundamentalism

The Rashtriya Swayamsevak Sangh (RSS) is a right-wing movement, whose members wear uniforms and exercise a certain military character. It identifies Hinduism with India itself and opposes secularism and other revisions and the setting up of a secular state. It, together with similar organizations, preaches a concept of 'Hindu-ness' known as *Hindutva*.

Hindu nationalists have gained a certain amount of ground through the political and electoral successes of the Bharatiya Janat Party (BJP), a party which managed to defeat the dominant Congress party in the 1998 elections and rule until 2004.

Linked to the RSS and the BJP is the Vishna Hindu Parishad (VHP), an organization made up of Hindu religious leaders. Many see the fundamentalist–nationalist alliance of these groups as a threat to the pluralistic face of such a diverse nation as India and fear the establishment of a theocratic state, where religious values and beliefs are regarded as the basis for national laws.

Reading guide to Hinduism

Brockington, J. L., *The Sacred Thread*: *Hinduism in its Continuity and Diversity*, University Press, Edinburgh, 1985 edn.

Flood, Gavin, *An Introduction to Hinduism*, Cambridge University Press, Cambridge, 1999 edn.

Kinsley, David R., *Hinduism: A Cultural Perspective,* Prentice-Hall, New Jersey, USA, 1982 edn.

Klostermaier, Klaus K., *Hindu Writings: A Short Introduction to the Major Sources*, Oneworld, Oxford, 2000.

Klostermaier, Klaus K., *Hinduism: A Short History,* Oneworld, Oxford, 2000.

Klostermaier, Klaus K., *Hinduism: A Short Introduction,* Oneworld, Oxford, 2005 edn.

Knott, Kim, *Hindusim: A Very Short Introduction*, Oxford University Press, Oxford, 2000 edn.

Olivelle, Patrick, *Upanishads*, Oxford University Press, Oxford, 1998 edn.

Parrinder, Geoffrey, *Avatar and Incarnation*, Faber and Faber, London, 1970.

Singh, Dharam Vir, *Hinduism: An Introduction*, Travel Wheels, Jaipur, India, 1995 edn.

Zaehner, R. C., *Hinduism*, Oxford University Press, Oxford, 1988 edn.

Jainism

History and Development

Jainism ranks with Hinduism and Buddhism as one of the most important of the ancient religions of the Indian sub-continent. It worships no supreme deity, but its followers revere a long line of *Tirthankaras* (meaning 'bridge-builder', 'ford-maker' or 'pathfinder'), also known as *Jinas*, from which the religion takes its name. The term *Jina* means 'conqueror'. This refers to their overcoming of human passion.

Size Of the estimated 4–6 million Jains worldwide the vast majority live in India, where they make up less than 0.5 per cent of the population.

Founder In recorded history, Mahavira.

Location Established in the sixth century BCE in India, either in the area of the Ganges Basin or the modern-day state of Bihar.

Western writers often characterize Mahavira as the founder of Jainism. Although this is not strictly true, he has had considerable influence on the religion. Jains view him as a significant figure in a long line of distinguished teachers. The *Tirthankaras* are believed to be enlightened religious teachers. Jainism teaches that the principles of the faith are taught by these holy teachers, who have themselves been set free from the cycle of endless birth and rebirth or *samsara*, having attained enlightenment. Jainism understands these teachers as fitting into a complicated chronology of cosmic cycles.

The cycle of the *Tirthankaras*

Jain cosmology (its philosophy of how the universe originated and developed) divides time into different cycles. Jains associate twenty-four *Jinas* or *Tirthankaras* with the last cosmic cycle. The last of these *Tirthankaras* was Mahavira. He is thought by historians to have died around 425 BCE, placing him around the latter part of the Vedic era. He is thought to have been a contemporary of Gautama Buddha.

Jain identity

Following the death of Mahavira, when the followers of Jainism were concentrated mostly in the north-east of India, many different groups of ascetics emerged, both monks and nuns, travelling about seeking alms and begging food.

With the influence of the wandering ascetics the faith spread rapidly. Many sects or orders emerged. Of all these the most significant were the *Svetambaras*, mainly in northern India, and the *Digambaras*, who are mainly to be found in the south.

In its historical development the spread and influence of Jainism was greatly helped by royal patronage. This was true for both main branches of the religion.

Although figures vary widely, it is estimated that there are now between 4 and 6 million Jains worldwide, the vast majority of them living in India, but suggestions for adherents can range as high as 10 million worldwide. The religion is numerically tiny in comparison to Hinduism, with Jains making up less than 0.5 per cent of India's population. Yet the influence of

At a temple in Gwalior in Madhya Pradesh, Central India, stand 15th-century sculptures of Jain *Tirthankaras* (bridge-builders).

Jainism in Indian society far outweighs its numerical strength and it has maintained continuity and adapted to its environment while keeping a distinct identity. Jainism places a strong emphasis on the sacredness of life. Its teachings continue to revolve around the principle of non-violence or *ahimsa*.

Founder and Significant Figures

In Jain tradition many teachers came before Mahavira. He is the final *Tirthankara* of twenty-four spiritual teachers. He became a perfect one through his victory over human passion and weakness. As a result he escaped from the cycle of rebirth.

The dates of his life and death are disputed. Most Jains believe he was born in 599 BCE as Nataputta Vardhamana and died in the village of Pavapur in Bihar state. Historians, however, differ widely as to the dates of his birth and death, and no accurate figures are available. He may have been born sometime in the 540s BCE and may have died anywhere between 477 BCE and 425 BCE, depending on the birth dates given. It is generally thought that he lived until he was 72- or 73-years-old.

Mahavira

Both orders of Jainism, the *Svetambaras* and the *Digambaras*, recognize the importance of Mahavira and claim their descent and authority from him. Both orders agree he was called Mahavira because he was fearless. In certain other aspects of his life their accounts differ.

◆ The *Svetambaras* believe he died in 527

Right: A hand-carved white marble statue of Mahavira in the Chandraprabhu Jain temple inside Jaisalmer Fort, Rajasthan, India.

BCE. The *Digambaras* insist he died in 510 BCE.

◆ They differ as to his place of birth. One text, the *Kalpasutra*, says it was in the Ganges Basin in Kundagrama (which has never been pinpointed).

◆ In the *Svetambara* account, prior to his birth his mother, Trisala, was visited with fourteen dreams which told of what a special child he would be.

◆ The *Svetambaras* hold their own views on Mahavira's conception. They believe his father, Siddartha, was not his biological father, nor was Trisala his biological mother. Rather, a Brahmin couple, named Rsabhadatta and Devananda, conceived Mahavira. Then the king of the gods, Sakra, also known as Indra, took the embryo and transplanted it into the womb of Trisala. Siddartha, Trisala's husband, was a chieftain of the *Kshatriya* clan, a warrior people. Traditionally, the *Tirthankaras* are born into the *Kshatriya* caste, and the story may represent an attempt to gain some superiority of the *Kshatriyas* over the *Brahmins.*

The life of Mahavira

Jains put a great deal of stress on Mahavira's ascetic development prior to his attainment of enlightenment. While Mahavira's predecessors are not well documented, he himself has received a great deal of attention in sacred texts.

◆ In *Svetambara* teaching, Mahavira married Yasoda, a princess, and they had a daughter, Priyadarsana. Once he reached the age of thirty, Mahavira began his period of renunciation. He tore out his hair in five handfuls and became an ascetic wanderer. After a period of thirteen months his clothing had disintegrated and the remnants of it were torn away by a thorn bush, leaving him to wander naked.

◆ The *Digambaras* deny that Mahavira ever married. They deny that he would ever have been a householder or a property owner and believe that the gods divested him of his clothing,

intending him to be a naked ascetic.

Mahavira travelled for a period of twelve years and Jain writings have references to his visiting many villages. In all of this time he was in search of enlightenment and the escape from *karma*. Finally he achieved the enlightenment which he had sought. Following this, he gathered a large number of disciples to himself. The accounts of the *Svetambaras* and *Digambaras* differ in the precise details, but Mahavira is said to have attracted many thousands of monks, nuns, laymen, and laywomen.

Branches of Jainism

An important feature of the historical development of Jainism was the divergence between two orders of Jain monks.

Svetambaras **and** Digambaras

The most significant of the emergenent sects were the *Svetambaras* and the *Digambaras.* As we have seen, there are many minor theological and doctrinal differences between these orders of monks, but the chief point of divergence lies in differing interpretations of what renunciation means in practice.

◆ The 'white-clad' *Svetambaras* wear white clothes. The *Digambaras* are known as 'the sky-clad ones' because they regard clothes as evidence of attachment to worldly values and inconsistent with an ascetic life; their clothes are simply the air.

◆ The *Svetambaras* accept religious women as nuns. Because the *Digambaras*

Jain monks walk down the steps in one of the most important Jain pilgrimage centres at Shravanabelagola, some 158 km (99 miles) west of the southern Indian city of Bangalore. The statue at the top of the steps – at 17 m (58 ft) high – is said to be the world's largest monolithic statue. Every 12 years, thousands of people come to Shravanabelagola for the Mahamastakabhisheka, when the statue is bathed with precious stones, milk, yogurt, saffron, and gold coins. It is a tradition that began in 981 CE.

believe that only men are allowed to go naked, this branch does not admit women into the religious life.

◆ The *Svetambaras* believe women can achieve liberation as *Tirthankaras*. The *Digambaras* disagree, because of the notion that during the menstrual cycle many micro-organisms are killed in the woman's body. The karmic result means that liberation cannot be achieved. To become a *Tirthankara*, they teach, a woman would need to be reborn as a man.

Sacred Writings

Following the death of Mahavira, his teachings were gathered and written down by his closest disciples. The preaching of any *Tirthankara* is greatly valued and revered. The early Jains used an ancient scriptural language known as Ardhamagadhi to record this teaching in a canon of scriptures known as the *agama*. However, while the *Svetambaras* understood that the sacred teachings of the *Tirthankaras* could be expressed in human language, the *Digambaras* hold that the original teachings of each *Tirthankara* are heard as the sacred syllable *om* (the sacred sound which contains within it powerful reverberations; in Jainism, the sound is also associated with the five *parameshtis*, or five enlightened beings to whom Jains pray every day. The 'Om' is elongated to encompass syllables which stand for each of the *parameshtis*) and then need to be deciphered and interpreted and written down. As a result there is no one single sacred text for the Jains. The *Svetambaras* and *Digambaras* differ as to which books should be regarded as sacred. The very earliest texts, the fourteen *purvas*, are believed by both groupings to have been lost in antiquity. To what extent later scriptures accurately reflect the teachings of this earliest text is a matter for dispute amongst Jains:

◆ In the *Svetambara* tradition, Mahavira's teachings are contained in a text known as 'the twelve-limbed basket of the disciples' or *duvalasamgaganipidaga*, and they believe that their own scriptures originate from and descend from this text.

◆ *Digambaras* assert that two important scriptural collections were lost in the second century BCE. At this time, another text was being compiled, the 'scripture of six parts', or *satkhandagama*, which contained within it essential elements of the original *purvas*. The *Digambaras*

Initiation into the ascetic life

The ceremony of initiation[1] into Jain ascetic life is known as *diksha*. It is considered to be on a par with marriage for the non-ascetic, since it binds the monk or nun to the ascetic community in much the same way. The ceremony differs across the various strands of Jainism. In the *Digambara* tradition, the ceremony is simple. The candidate will leave his parents, abandon his clothing, pull out his hair, and take his vows, along with a new name. His body is painted with symbols in the way a sacred image might be painted, to indicate consecration and dedication.

For the *Digambara* and *Svetambara* Jains, a preliminary period is recommended before acceptance into formal ordination into the ascetic life. For the *Svetambaras*, this is known as the 'little' *diksha*. After expressing a desire to enter into the ascetic life, the candidate is often given a new name and then required to participate in a probationary period of a month. For some sects of the *Svetambara*, the probationary period may last for up to two years. During this period, the prospective ascetic must engage in prayer and fasting. The *Digambara* probationary period offers two routes into the ascetic life for those who do not wish to be fully initiated. For those male ascetics who do not wish to take full vows and go naked, there is the option of becoming a *kshullaka*, which means 'lesser' and which involves the wearing of a robe. The *kshullaka* does not have to shave his head and is allowed to bathe. He may also have a bowl to beg for alms. The other option, which is above the status of a *kshullaka*, is to become a partially clothed ascetic or *ailaka*. This candidate wears a loincloth but may not carry a begging bowl. The *ailaka* must also pull out his hair and is not allowed to wash.

When the *Svetambara* is ready to take full vows, or 'big' *diksha*, the hair is either pulled out or the head may be shaved and a certain amount of hair left in tufts to be pulled out. A robe is given to the candidate, along with a whisk for brushing away insects and an alms bowl for begging. For *Digambaras*, only adults can be initiated into the ascetic life, but *Svetambaras* may accept candidates who are as young as eight years old.

Two Indian Jain monks walk barefoot along the promenade in Bombay. Jain monks spread word of the Jain religion, preaching peace and non-violence.

also value *The treatise on the passions* or *Kasayaprabhrta*, written by a sage and ascetic named Gunabhadra.

The *Svetambara* canon

The standard *Svetambara* canon of scripture consists of forty-five texts. These are grouped into twelve *angas* or 'limbs'. The twelfth *anga* has been lost and is believed to have consisted of the teachings of the lost *purvas*.

The scriptures cover a wide variety of topics. The *Acaranga Sutra* covers the issue of good conduct, the *Sutrakrtanga* deals with the views of rival religious schools, while the *Antakrddasahanga* tells the stories of those holy figures who have managed to end the cycle of *samsara*.

There are twelve subsidiary *angas* alongside the twelve main *angas*, and these are known as the *upangas*. Some branches of the *Svetambara* accept only thirty-two texts. There is some difficulty in definitively establishing the number of *Svetambara* scriptures. The canon of texts which was supposedly set after the Council of Valabhi in the mid-sixth century CE is nowhere set out as a list of individual texts, so the canon accepted today may be of a much later date, finalized in the thirteenth

A Jain nun prays at the feet of the monolithic statue of Gomateshwara in Shravanabelagola.

century CE. Scripture is revered and many temples are dedicated to sacred texts.

The *Digambara* canon

The *Digambaras* do not hold to the *Svetambara* canon. In the *Digambara* tradition, scripture takes on a metaphorical rather than a literal role. This is probably because they believe that the most illuminating scriptures were lost very soon after the death of Mahavira. As has been said, the *Digambaras* accept as scriptural the 'scripture of six parts' and *The treatise on the passions*. Some *Digambaras* do accept the validity of certain *Svetambara* scriptures, but they are very selective.

Jains believe that in general, lay people should not seek to interpret the scriptures for themselves as they may lack the specialist skills needed. Monks are usually the authorities in scriptural teaching and interpretation.

Core Beliefs

Karma, samsara, moksha

A central feature of Jain belief is the notion of *karma* – meaning 'action' – which refers to the outcome of human action and the impact on one's life which this action can have. Jains differ somewhat from Hindus in their understanding of what *karma* is.

In Jain teaching *karma* is physical matter. The soul which is alive with passion and desire attracts *karma* almost as a pollutant: *karma* sticks to this type of soul and the soul becomes trapped in a form of bondage. In certain cases bad *karma* can completely obscure a

soul, turning it a dark colour, which has very negative connotations. Intentional bad action is differentiated from non-intentional harmful action, and the intent to do evil can have a significantly negative effect on the result of *karma*. The overall consequence of *karma* is to trap the soul in the continuous cycle of *samsara* and to prevent it from attaining freedom, or *moksha*.

The enlightenment that needs to be experienced for *moksha* is linked to omniscience. *Karma* keeps the soul in ignorance and prevents it from seeing all knowledge. Omniscience is to know and understand everything. It is a mystical experience and begins with knowing one's own inner nature. It then looks outward to become a knowledge of the whole of the universe and of existence. *Karma* is extremely important because it explains why human beings demonstrate a variety of different life experiences and why some lives appear to have greater quality and meaning than others. The human soul is able to make decisions as to how it will respond to life's challenges, but these decisions can have eternal consequences.

The issue of freedom from the bondage of *samsara* is a core aspect of belief in Jainism. Each individual human being has to accept personal responsibility for his or her journey of liberation.

The concept of God

Jains do not believe in a creator God; they offer veneration and worship to enlightened beings. They do not believe a god figure intervenes in human affairs.

However, the Jain concept of *paramatman* or the 'supreme self' can be understood as a 'divine principle' which lives within all beings. Those liberated souls who have achieved this state are revered by Jains. The *Tirthankaras* or 'bridge-builders', taken as a corporate body of enlightened beings, are commonly thought of as 'God'.

The Three Jewels

The journey to liberation is aided by practising what are known as the 'three jewels'. The first jewel or *samyak darshana* is associated with the achievement of correct insight, which involves both the desire to live by religious principles and the attainment of light provided by the inspiration of a spiritual revelation. The believer then needs correct knowledge or *samyak jnana*, to guide the way along the path, and *samyak carira*, which is right conduct and behaviour.

Jain cosmology

Jain cosmology, or its philosophy of how the universe is constructed, divides into three main areas, each of which has several subdivisions. Firstly, there is the underworld; secondly, the earthly world; thirdly, the heavenly realm. Above these worlds, beyond the heavenly realm, is the place where the enlightened ones live. These enlightened or liberated souls are treated as divinities; although Jainism does not have a belief in a single supreme being, it does give worship to these.

There are many different layers in the Jains' concept of the universe. Different beings live at various levels, according to their karmic status. The entire universe is known as the *loka*. The Jains believe that the universe is uncreated: it does not have a beginning and it will not have an end. Even the Hindu deities, *Brahma* and *Vishnu*, are subject to the laws of *karma* and *samsara* in Jain teaching. The middle layer, that which is concerned with the earth and human life, is the most important of all because it is the abode of humanity – the only beings who are capable of attaining enlightenment. In reality the Jain view of the universe is extraordinarily complex. It also proposes a geography of the world that is unrecognizable to modern humanity. As a result, many Jains accept it as a symbolic representation of the way the universe is structured.

Existence

According to Jain teaching, all physical objects exist in three aspects. They have the state of *dravya* or 'substance', *gunas* or 'qualities which are inherent to the object', and *paryayas*, 'the ability to change'. Matter is in a constant state of change and flux. It is both permanent and impermanent. Although objects may appear not to change during the short time in which they are being observed by us, they are in fact in a continual state of transformation. Therefore, within Jain belief, there is a reluctance to be dogmatic, as there are many different ways of seeing any object, situation or concept and everything is in a state of transition.

Jains believe that all living beings have souls. In the Jain concept of what constitutes reality, there is that which is composed of matter and there are sentient beings, which have souls. The soul, Jains believe, has always experienced bondage and has never known true liberation, but this can be remedied by following the path which leads to *moksha*. Souls can exist in many different forms and at many different levels, and not only in humans. They may even exist in plants and animals. Some inhabit heavenly beings; others are the souls of beings which inhabit the hellish realms. There are, Jains believe, many tiny, imperceptible, life forms, all of which have souls but which have been

A masked Jain nun blesses temple idols with sandalwood, Parsavanath Swami Jain Temple, Bangalore, South India.

born at the lowest level possible. There are even beings which are made up of either earth, fire, water or air. These exist at the most basic level as part of the constituent basis of all matter. At death, the soul is reincarnated into another body, although not necessarily the same kind of body as the previous incarnation. It is because each human soul may once have existed as any one of any number of other possible incarnations that Jains give great respect to all living things. It is also possible that the human soul may be reborn into a lower existence next time round.

Worship and Festivals

An important feature of Jain worship is the worship or *puja* directed towards images of

The Five Practices[2]

Ahimsa (Non-violence)

Out of its reverence for all living things, Jainism places an emphasis on non-violence or *ahimsa*. It is a fundamental part of Jain belief that all living beings are capable of experiencing suffering. Harming any living thing can cause extremely negative karmic effects. One important consequence of this belief is that Jains are vegetarian. Jains also avoid any unnecessary eating of plant life. As a result, fasting is a central feature of Jain religious practice.

When Jain ascetics travel, they employ a soft broom to sweep the ground before them free of any small creatures or organisms, lest they inadvertently tread on them. Some Jain monks, particularly those of the *Terapanthi* and *Sthanakvasi* sects of the *Svetambaras*, cover their nose and mouth with a cloth shield to prevent them from inhaling any tiny organisms in the air or harming them with their breath. There are Jain ascetics who will not go outside on rainy days in case they harm creatures that live in the water. Dietary restrictions make the issue of food very problematic. Foods which grow under the ground or *zamikand*, such as root vegetables, are forbidden because it is believed that millions of tiny creatures live in the earth and these are destroyed when the vegetables are harvested. It is also thought that the vegetables themselves contain micro-organisms. Jains boil water before they drink it to ensure that no living organisms are consumed. In some circumstances, bathing is kept to a minimum to spare the lives of any waterborne creatures.

Satya (Truthfulness)

Telling the truth or *satya* is important to Jains, who are expected to be honest in their dealings with others and in business transactions. Where telling the truth would cause offence or promote violence, Jains believe silence is preferable.

Asteya (Stealing)

In addition to not lying, Jains are expected to be honest with regard to their possessions and not engage in theft. This is known as *asteya*.

Brahmacaya (Sexual and moral purity)

Jains are expected to remain faithful to a spouse and not engage in sexual misconduct. Jain monks and nuns are required to remain celibate and refrain from sexual activity – a practice known as *brahmacaya*.

Aparigraha (Non-attachment and freedom)

Jains try to renounce attachment to worldly possessions and desires. Ascetics are thought to be able to achieve non-attachment to the highest degree, although even lay people are expected to practise restraint with regard to food, clothes and adornments, and possessions such as land and equipment. *Digambara* monks practise renunciation to the degree that they do not wear clothes. In their tradition, women may not become nuns or be seen naked and cannot attain liberation. In the *Svetambara* system women can become nuns. *Svetambaras* assert that the nineteenth *Tirthankara* was a woman.

the 'bridge-builders' or *Tirthankaras*. Most adherents of both the *Svetambara* and *Digambara* traditions worship images of the *Tirthankaras* (or *jinas*) in their temples, which are usually very richly decorated. *Puja* also takes place in the home and many Jain families keep small shrines. However, some numerically small sects reject any worship of the images of the bridge-builders. These include two sects of the *Svetambaras*, namely the *Terapanthis* and the *Sthanakvasis*, and the *Teranapanthi* sect of the *Digambara*.

Temple worship

Since Jains are expected to approach the

The Jain Temple of Ranakpur, Rajasthan, India.

The *puja* of eight substances

This ritual is practised in many different forms, usually in the morning after bathing. On entering the temple the worshipper should be in a state of purity. A *Svetambara* version would, broadly, follow these steps.

◆ The lay worshipper bows before the statue of the *Jina* and recites the word *nishi*, meaning 'abandonment'. With this act the Jain moves from the ordinary world into a sacred area.

◆ The worshipper walks around the image of the ford-maker three times in a clockwise direction, a circumambulation known as a *pradaksina*.

◆ Using substances brought from home and substances available in the temple, the worshipper first washes the image of the *Jina* and anoints it with a mixture of milk and water. *Gandh*, a mixture of camphor and sandalwood, is rubbed on the image.

◆ Garlands of flowers are offered to the *Jina*.

◆ In another area of the temple the worshipper offers incense and lamps towards the image and performs a dance of joy.

◆ While dancing, the worshipper may wave a yak-tail fan and look in a mirror.

◆ Then rice, sweets and fruit are offered. The rice is arranged on a plate in the shape of a *svastika*, a sign sacred to the Jains, the four corners of which stand for the four main forms of existence for the soul – human, animal, hell-being and god. Three dots are placed above the *svastika* to symbolize the three jewels, and above these a single dot as a reminder of those liberated beings who live above the universe. The worshipper leaves a small financial offering for temple use.

◆ The ceremony ends with the word *nishi* and contemplation and the saying of certain prayers.

This *puja* may be performed daily. The substances are not offerings in the sense of gifts (for which an ascetic *Jina* would have no use) but gestures of renunciation. The worship shows devotion. It does not appease the *Jinas* or win favours from them.

In the *Digambara* form of the ritual, flowers are placed before the image and prayers are said, but the images are not anointed.

Devotees look
on during the
Mahamastakabhisheka
of the monolithic statue
of Gomateshwara at
Shravanabelagola.

Tirthankaras without a mediator, worship
at the temple tends to be individual, not
congregational. Worshippers approaching
puja strive to have the correct inner state
or *bhava*. The most common form of *puja*,
known as *darshana*, involves an act of
looking intently at the image with a strong
feeling of devotion.

Only lay Jains can anoint the sacred
images in an action known as *dravyapuja*.

This is because the ascetics are to concern
themselves solely with inner worship.

◆ *Digambara* monks delegate the
anointing of the images to a priest or
upadhye.

◆ In *Svetembara* temples lay people are
able to anoint the images, or temple
servants known as *pujari* may do so.

- The *Svetembara* like to adorn the images of the *Jinas* in fine clothing. The *Digambara* images are shown as being naked and are generally plain and free of embellishment.

Festivals

Jain rituals through the year include ascetic practices and festivals, most taking place at times determined by the phases of the moon. Fasting, as well as being a private devotion, can be carried out in groups and involves much ritual.

- Like Hindus, Jains celebrate *Diwali*, the festival of light. They use it to meditate on the enlightenment of Mahavira.

- *Paryushan*, a particularly *Svetambara* festival, celebrates the end of the old year. It lasts 8–10 days around August–September and involves a ritual forgiveness of sin, known as *pratikramana*. Many Jains send cards to friends and relatives, asking for forgiveness for any wrongs committed.

- *Dasha Lakshana Parvan* is celebrated by the *Digambaras* just after *Paryushan*. It is a very similar festival. However, different religious texts are used.

- The birthday of Mahavira is celebrated between March and April.

- *Akshaya Tritiya*, in April–May, is celebrated by both traditions. It involves fasting and a pilgrimage to Mount Satrunjaya in Gujarat.

Family and Society

Because of the importance of the ascetic life in Jainism, Jain society takes special account of the categories of monks, nuns, laymen, and laywomen. These are the four main divisions or *tirthas* in Jain society.

Monks, nuns, and laity

Many splits have occurred over interpretations of Mahavira's teachings, with Jain adherents ascribing allegiance to various groupings. This is further complicated by problems with caste. Differences, then, can be both sociological and religious.

The main sects, the *Digambaras* and the *Svetambaras*, are divided by the issue of possessions and the use of clothing, the former renouncing even that (see pp. 115–117).

Ascetics are very highly regarded and are important, highly visible members of the community. On meeting an ascetic, a lay Jain will bow twice and say a short prayer of veneration. Ascetics teach lay people about religious matters and offer spiritual counsel. Lay people, in turn, increase karmic virtue by providing for the ascetics. Within Jain religious life, nuns are regarded as being inferior to monks and they must show monks due deference and respect. Within ascetic communities, there exists a strict hierarchy, with the head of the order, the *acharya*, at the apex.

Caste

Caste is an important issue for Jains, although Mahavira did not accept the

One of the many symbols of the Jain faith. The Jain hand tells adherents to stop and reflect. Here this sacred symbol is stenciled on a hand-painted canvas.

Some key terms

Sikh has Sanskrit roots and means 'disciple'. In Punjabi, it carries the meaning 'to learn'. Thus, a Sikh is one who is following a path and who is learning on the journey in a continuous act of religious discipleship.

Singh, which means 'lion', is the standard surname for Sikh men.

Kaur, meaning 'princess', is the surname employed by Sikh women.

Right: Turban of a Nihang (an armed Sikh order) with Sikh symbols. This man is attending the Vaisakhi harvest festival in the Takht Sri Damdama Sahib in Talwandi Sabo (Punjab, India).

did not offer devotion to the *avatars* or incarnations of Vishnu, but they believed in a direct approach to Vishnu himself and direct union with him through meditative practices. However, they tried to transcend social distinctions and ritualistic observances.

Just as *Sufis* concentrate on union with the divine and on the subsuming of the human soul into the great divine spirit, the *Sants* sang devotional hymns and recited the name of God in a repetitive manner, in order to gain closer union with him. One of the most important *Sant* poets was Kabir (probably 1440–1518 CE). He tried to bring Hindu and Muslim spirituality together and was considered a mystic.

Whereas earlier Muslim leaders had sought to convert what were regarded as the polytheistic Hindus to monotheism, those who subscribed to the *Sant* traditions were able to view Hinduism and Islam not as mutually exclusive, but in places as complementary. For example, the Muslim focus on monotheism did not risk being compromised if the Hindu concept of an overarching being, behind all of the manifestations of Hindu deities, was recognized. This *Brahman* could be viewed as a single God who revealed himself in many ways. It was within this context of the interaction of both Hindu and Muslim spiritual traditions that Guru Nanak developed his own spiritual approach which led to the path known as Sikhism. The emergence of Sikhism owed a great deal to the *Sant* movement.

Today Sikhs are found all over the world and large communities of Sikhs exist in

the UK, North America, and East Africa. A substantial number of Sikhs serve in India's armed forces and achieve high ranks. Sikh men may be recognized by the colourful turbans they wear. However, a turban over uncut hair is only one of the five religious symbols traditionally worn by Sikh men (see p. 132).

Founder and Significant Figures

Guru Nanak (1469–1539)

Nanak was born into a Hindu family in the Punjab, members of the *kshatriya* class, often associated with warriors and rulers. His father was an accountant; his mother had a reputation for holiness and religious practice. As has been noted, the Punjab was a place of some diversity, both cultural and religious. Its position as the place which had to do most to defend itself against invaders meant that its people were

tough and independent, ready to stand up for their ideals.

The most important source for Nanak's life is the *Janam Sakhis* or 'birth stories', written about a hundred years after his death, although preserved before that in oral transmission. In the writings of the *Janam Sakhis* the story is told of how, even at a very young age, Nanak was preoccupied with the things of God. He explored the teachings of both Hinduism and Islam, but found greatest light in the teachings of the *Sants*. Following marriage at the age of nineteen to Sulakhani, he moved with his new wife to the town of Sultanpur. His search for spiritual truth deepened and he obtained work in administration. Having met many Muslims, and those of other beliefs, Nanak was now seeking out the company of spiritually minded people. One of these was a Muslim minstrel named Mardana. With Mardana

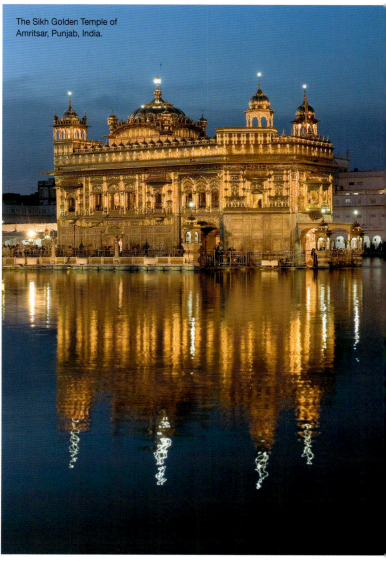

The Sikh Golden Temple of Amritsar, Punjab, India.

The Five Ks

Five emblems were established by Guru Gobind Singh in 1699, when he instituted the *Khalsa* or the 'Pure Ones'. These symbols mark out Sikh identity in a very distinct way. Five forms of dress identify the initiated male members of the *Khalsa*.

◆ *Kes*, uncut hair and beard, which is kept in place by a turban.

◆ *Kangha*, a comb worn in the hair which distinguishes the Sikh from those Indian holy men who keep unkempt hair.

◆ *Kirpan*, a short sword which reminds the Sikh that he must defend the weak.

◆ *Kara*, a steel bracelet symbolizing the unity of God; worn on the right wrist.

◆ *Kachhas* (also known as *kachs*), baggy shorts which symbolize readiness for action and spiritual freedom.

The Sikh emblem – the *khanda* – comprises the *khanda* itself (a dagger which stands for the twin concepts of freedom and justice), the *chakar*, a circle to represent unity, and two *kirpans* or short swords which represent religious and temporal power.

Not all Sikhs are initiated into the *Khalsa*, but many who are not do still wear their hair uncut and in a turban.

Branches of Sikhism

Kesdhari Sikhs follow almost all of the *Khalsa* tradition, but do not cut their hair and do not go through an initiation ceremony. Sikhs who do not aspire to or do not reach the full grade of *Khalsa* are known as *Shahajdhari* Sikhs. These Sikhs cut their hair. *Udasis* are Sikhs who set themselves apart by opting for a celibate and ascetic life. They also cut their hair.

Sacred Writings

In 1604 the fifth Guru, Arjan, compiled the Sikhs' principal scripture: the *Adi Granth* or 'original book'. It included the hymns of the first four Gurus together with some by Guru Arjan.

Guru Granth Sahib

The highly revered *Adi Granth* became known as *Guru Granth Sahib* or *Sri Guru Granth Sahib* – a *guru* being a teacher, *granth* meaning 'book' and *sri* and *sahib* being titles of respect, rather like 'sir' and 'lord'. The first Guru, Nanak, had left many sacred songs and hymns, believed to have been given to him directly by God. Subsequent Gurus added their own hymns to the community's store of sacred songs, each one of them stressing the continuity with Nanak's works. In addition, the *Guru Granth Sahib* contains the writings of Hindu and Muslim holy men whose contributions were revered by the Sikh community, men such as the poets Kabir, Namdev, and Ramidas.

Arjan put the hymns in order of the line of Gurus before him. He also arranged them musically, so that poems having the same melodic patterns and rhythms are held together. All in all, he arranged the *Adi Granth* into thirty-one sections. The

The 'onkar' symbol meaning 'God is One' can be found in a Sikh temple.

Adi Granth or *Guru Granth Sahib* was placed in the Golden Temple at Amritsar.

Initially the *Adi Granth* was handwritten in a form of the Punjabi language, *Gurmukhi*, the term meaning 'from the guru's mouth'. Eventually permission was given to print it. Every copy must be identical to the extent that identical information is to be found on each page. All copies must be the same length: 1,430 pages. However, when printed in other languages the same length cannot be maintained, owing to differences in script and phraseology.

The *Guru Granth Sahib* has a very special authority, since it replaces the role of the human Guru. It is used extensively at Sikh gatherings and is often read continuously as a way of giving blessing. In the temple or *gurdwara* it is kept on a raised platform underneath a canopy and is fanned during worship with a ritual fan. The *Guru Granth Sahib* opens with the words '*Ek Onkar*' which refer to the oneness of God. Literally, it means: 'There is one God.' It immediately directs the Sikh's eyes to the central truth of the faith and sets the context for the rest of the book. It is the Sikh affirmation of faith.

Dasam Granth

Another important scripture for the Sikhs, but which does not have the same status as the *Guru Granth Sahib*, is the *Dasam Granth*. Compiled in 1734, some twenty-six years after the death of the final human Guru, Gobind Singh, it contains compositions by him and some other poets. Gobind Singh had added

A page from the *Guru Granth Sahib*.

some compositions to the *Adi Granth* by his father, the ninth Guru, but none of his own. The *Dasam Granth* is 1,428 pages long. *Gurdwaras* are not expected to keep a copy of the *Dasam* in the same way that they do the *Guru Granth Sahib*, but it can be used in some ceremonies.

Core Beliefs

The opening words of the principal Sikh scripture – *Ek Onkar* – not only refer to one God, but also attribute to this God important characteristics which determine his relationship with creation.

The concept of God

At the centre of Sikhism is a belief in one God. This God can be directly experienced in the human soul. God is thought of as the

Sikhs attend the Sarbat Khalsa Sikh convention after the Indian prime minister sent troops into the Sikh holy temple, the Golden Temple in Amritsar. The Sarbat Khalsa is a meeting of all Sikhs to consider important *Panth* issues.

absolute. He is without form and is eternal. He is immanent in the human soul, but is also transcendent, being above and beyond time. The human being may attain a union with this God, however. He is not far away, but desires fellowship with human beings. He is truth, creator, love. He is immortal and eternal and self-illuminated and is revealed through the *Guru Granth Sahib* and the teachings of the ten Gurus.

It is possible for a human being to have direct access to God and this access can be gained in the human soul. Sikhism emphasizes a very personal relationship with God and acknowledges an ultimate truth which lies behind every religious path, no matter how diverse. The *Guru Granth Sahib* speaks of the will of God or *hukam*. This also refers to the order which is upheld in the universe by the divine will.

Without it, nothing could exist or continue to exist.

Karma and *mukti*

Sikhism accepts the concept of reincarnation and believes in the idea of *karma*. It acknowledges the existence of the *samsara* or cycle of birth and death, but calls this cycle *awagaun*. At death the eternal soul either becomes one with the divine or transmigrates into another living form, depending on the outcome of one's *karma*.

There is a strong tradition of the grace of God in Sikhism. This grace is called by a Persian word, *nadar*. It means to have divine favour. It is able to break the cycle of death and rebirth.

As a result, the Sikh is never entirely at the mercy of a determined cycle, driven by *karma*. The Sikh can attain liberation or *mukti*, which means the same as the Hindu Sanskrit term, *moksha*. Part of this liberation can be achieved through following the teachings of the *Guru Granth Sahib* and the ten human Gurus.

A Sikh must serve God and lead a virtuous life through practising three central requirements:

◆ The Sikh must practise *nam japna*, which is meditation on the name of God.

◆ *Kirt karma* is the duty of work to support oneself; the Sikh must be honest and work in an honest occupation.

◆ *Vand chakna* is the duty to help and support others in fellowship and charity.

The bhog ceremony

The word *bhog* can be translated as 'pleasure'. The *bhog* ceremony[1] consists of the reading of the final pages of the *Guru Granth Sahib* and the participation in the Sikh sacrament of eating *Karah prasad*, a sweet food. *Bhog* does not have to take place in the *gurdwara*, but can take place anywhere and can be led by any member of the Sikh community. It takes place around the *Guru Granth Sahib*, which everyone faces. *Karah prasad* is then prepared. The sacramental food is made up of butter, flour and sugar in equal parts and it is cooked while the congregation remains in an attitude of prayer. The participants will cover their heads and sit barefoot on the floor singing hymns from the *Guru Granth Sahib*. The *Karah prasad* is then put into a flat dish and covered. Next, it is placed on the right of the *Guru Granth Sahib*.

As well as the singing of hymns from the *Guru Granth Sahib*, the last five pages of the sacred text are chanted aloud by a reader. After this, the congregation stands and recites the *ardas*, which is a prayer of petition. In this prayer, Sikhs call to mind the Ultimate Reality (that is, God, who is one reality and who can be known by human beings – in Sikhism this God is known as Ik (or Ek) Onkar, a title which literally means 'One God'), the first ten gurus, and the way in which the *Guru Granth Sahib* reflects their teachings. The *ardas* concludes with the congregation praying for the whole of humanity. The people bow in front of the holy book, with their foreheads touching the ground. Then they sit in front of it. At this point, whoever is leading the service will open the *Guru Granth Sahib* and recite the hymn on the top left-hand side of the page which he or she has opened. This is then considered to be a reading of instruction for that particular day.

At the end of all this, the congregation partakes of the *Karah prasad*, receiving it in the palms of their hands. Following the distribution of the *Karah prasad*, the community may then take part in the community meal known as the *langar*.

By following these goals, the Sikh becomes less self-focused and more focused on the teachings of the Gurus. This is called *gursikhi* or 'Guru-focused'. As a result of this, the Sikh is able to fight against the 'Five thieves':

terms of kinship groups or birth groups. Sikh weddings generally follow Indian custom, but the ceremony is held in the *gurdwara* and the *Guru Granth Sahib* plays an important religious role in this.

Death

Sikh funerals follow the general Indian custom of cremation. After the body is washed and clothed, it is dressed in the Five Ks and taken to a funeral pyre. Hymns are sung and the ashes will be scattered in some holy place or in a sacred river.

Birth and name-giving

Birth and naming rites are big social occasions. Other Sikhs will visit the family and bring gifts. It is more usual to celebrate the birth of a boy than that of a girl, so the celebrations for the birth of a girl are more muted. At the name-giving ceremony in the *gurdwara*, the *Guru Granth Sahib* will be read. It will be opened at random and the first letter on the page opened will be chosen to be the first letter of the child's name. Boys are given the title *Singh*, which means 'lion'. Girls receive the title *Kaur* or 'princess'.

Contemporary Issues

Sikhism has become increasingly politicized, especially in India. Under British rule, many reform movements grew up within Sikhism to spiritually sustain a people who were suffering politically. These movements strengthened Sikh identity, which became quite distinct from Hinduism. It was a time rich in literature and in theology for the Sikh faith.

Independence or autonomy?

Following the partition of India in 1947, Sikhs on the Muslim side of the Punjab in Pakistan resettled on the Indian side of the border, strengthening their number and influence. In the 1980s, anxious for their own political homeland, Sikhs found themselves at odds with the Indian government and armed forces and this resulted in some considerable tension and bloodshed. In 1984, as an act of retaliation for her role in ordering Indian troops to storm the Golden Temple at Amritsar, the Indian Prime Minister Indira Gandhi was assassinated by her Sikh bodyguards.

Women in Sikhism

Guru Nanak viewed women as part of divine creation. They were not viewed by him in negative terms, as sources of uncleanness or pollution. However, as in many other religions, men traditionally fulfil the authority roles and positions of leadership within the community. Although the *Guru Granth Sahib* teaches that women are not inferior, and women have a distinguished role in Sikh history, there is often a gulf between teaching and practice.

The Sikh diaspora

There is a strong Sikh diaspora, with many Sikhs moving overseas. Sikhs in India are usually seen as prosperous and many are involved in the professional and business classes. Statistics for the Indian state of Punjab, where Sikhs make up nearly two-thirds of the population, show a higher

Sikh reform movements

In the second half of the nineteenth century, Sikhs felt particularly disempowered in directing their own destiny as a result of British rule in India. Various reform movements[2] emerged during this period and each one helped to more sharply define Sikh identity at a time of change and uncertainty.

The Nirankaris, founded by Dyal Das (1783–1853), were so called because their name meant 'worshippers of the Formless One'. Dyal Das condemned any worship of images and any participation in Hindu ritual by Sikhs. The Nirankaris were mainly concentrated around the Rawalpindi area. As well as revering the *Guru Granth Sahib*, the followers of Dyal Das also revered his own *Hukam-nma* or *Book of Ordinances*.

The Namdharis owed their foundation to Ram Singh (1816–84). This movement followed its own baptismal ritual and rule of life. Followers were expected to be strictly vegetarian and were encouraged to dress in all-white attire. A strong emphasis was placed on discipline and chanting. The name 'Namdhari' was given to the movement because of its commitment to the chanting of the divine name. Ram Singh was firmly against the practice of the slaughter of animals which had been allowed by the British, and in 1871 many Muslim butchers in Amritsar and Ludhiana were killed. British forces fiercely suppressed the Namdharis and exiled Ram Singh. The Namdharis believed that Guru Gobind Singh was not killed in 1708 but rather went into hiding, to be succeeded by Ram Singh. He is considered to be still alive and in hiding and his return is expected. The descendants of Ram Singh are considered to be his representatives in the meantime and they represent authority within the movement.

Opposite: Sikh men pray at a parade in Vancouver, Canada. The parade is for Visaki, a traditional Sikh celebration.

The judges' service at Westminster Abbey, London, UK, 2001. The procession of judges includes Sir Mota Singh, a Sikh judge who wears the turban.

Reading guide to Sikhism

Mann, Gurinder Singh, *Sikhism*, Prentice-Hall, New Jersey, 2004.

McLeod, W. H., *Guru Nanak and the Sikh Religion,* Oxford University Press, Oxford, 1968.

McLeod, W. H., *The Sikhs: History, Religion and Society,* Columbia University Press, New York, 1989.

McLeod, W. H., *Historical Dictionary of Sikhism,* Oxford University Press, New Delhi, 2002 edn.

Shackle, Christopher, *Teachings of the Sikh Gurus,* Routledge, London, 2005.

Singh, Gopal, *The Religion of the Sikhs,* Asia Publishing House, London, 1971.

Singh, Harbans, *Guru Nanak and the Origins of the Sikh Faith*, Asia Publishing House, Punjabi University, India, 1969.

Singh, Nikky-Guninder Kaur, *Sikhism*, Facts on File, New York, 1993.

Sri Guru Granth Sahib, An English Translation by Gurbachan Singh Talib, Volumes I & II, Publication Bureau, Punjab University, Pattiala, India, 1984, 1985.

average wage than elsewhere and the lowest rating for poverty. This ability to create prosperity has transferred to the Sikhs who moved abroad. The Sikh emphasis on fellowship has created strong and supportive communities in many parts of the world, including North America and the UK.

In the Western world Sikh scholars are re-examining many Sikh beliefs with a view to making the faith relevant in modern contexts. The distinctiveness of Sikh male dress in particular has led to some tension between Sikhs and the secular societies in which they live. In general Sikhs, with their history of pluralism and multiculturalism, are able to adapt well to the environments in which they find themselves.

Buddhism

History and Development

It is thought that 'the Buddha' or 'the enlightened one' – the founder of Buddhism – was born in northern India in the sixth or fifth century BCE. One chronology places his birth around 490 BCE; others suggest around 560 BCE.

Buddhists try to place an emphasis on the teaching of the Buddha, rather than on the Buddha himself. The *dharma*, or the path that the Buddha taught his disciples to follow, is viewed as the vehicle of truth.

There is some debate as to whether Buddhism can be classed as a religion, with many viewing it more as a philosophy or a code of ethics. The absence of the idea of a creator God is problematic for some in interpreting Buddhism as a religion, while others see no contradiction in regarding it as a non-theistic religion.

Emerging in northern India
During the period of the Buddha's lifetime religious developments in northern India had led to much spiritual questioning. The concepts of *karma* and rebirth were already established features of religious thought and society was organized along the caste system. Many were opting for the ascetic life in an effort to gain deeper spiritual understanding, causing tension between those seeking enlightenment in this way and those who followed the teaching and ritualistic practices of the Brahmin priests. The roots of the Buddhist religion, then, lie in the Hindu tradition.

When Siddartha Gautama – later to be called the Buddha or Shakyamuni, the 'sage' or 'wise one' – achieved

Size With approximately 350 million adherents, Buddhism is one of the largest religious groupings in the world.

Founder Siddartha Gautama (the Buddha).

Location Originating in India in the sixth century or fifth century BCE and spreading rapidly eastward, as far as China, Japan, and Indonesia, Buddhism now has adherents in the West numbering upwards of 4 million.

enlightenment and set out to teach it, he converted many ascetics to his message. The result of his preaching was the establishment of a community or order into which women as well as men could be inducted, known as the *sangha*. This became an important vehicle for spreading Buddhism's influence. Monks and nuns exercise a valuable role within Buddhism and are revered for their way of life and their teaching example.

A path with different styles

Having himself reached the state of nirvana or pure enlightenment, Gautama Buddha was the originator of the spiritual path which Buddhists follow to arrive at a similar state. Indeed the term 'Buddha' is not a personal name, but a title that shows where the path is leading, for what Buddhists are interested in attaining is a state of 'Buddha-hood' wherein enlightenment can be experienced.

Buddhists share a common goal, but one of the Buddha's legacies was the precise instruction that his teachings should not be tied to any single doctrinal interpretation. This lack of need for a strict adherence to a rigid doctrine laid down by an immutable authority gives Buddhism flexibility. As a result, various groupings emphasize different aspects of what it means to be Buddhist, allowing Buddhism to adapt well to the different cultures and societies into which it has been transplanted, particularly in its more contemporary manifestations. This is especially true in the West, where significant elements of Buddhism have been incorporated into Western spiritualities.

Opposite: A Buddha statue lit up at the Loi Krathong festival.

Branching out

Buddhism initially spread throughout India and into Sri Lanka, then to countries to the east, sometimes establishing communities, in other cases prompting local religions to review their beliefs or practices. Buddhism helped to reshape other religions and was reshaped itself.

Within about a hundred years of the Buddha's death, serious disagreements emerged. Following splits within the movement, two traditions were created that established lasting influence. They continue to be the main branches of Buddhism today: the *Theravada*, which is a monastic tradition, and the *Mahayana*.

In India, where Buddhism began, it has suffered a historic decline, although different branches continue to practise. In the 1890s a revivalist form of Buddhism took root amongst the *dalits*. The *dalits* comprise the lowest caste in India. Many even regard them to be so lowly as to be outside of the caste system. Many *dalits*, as a result of prejudice, have opted to become Buddhists in an attempt to have better and more meaningful lives. Numbers converting to Buddhism increased following the conversion of a prominent *dalit*, B. R. Ambedkar in 1956. However, the move towards Buddhism was already popular since the 1890s.

More recently an influx of Tibetan exiles into the country has led to increased activity in the Dharamsala area.

Founder and Significant Figures

The overarching figure in every variety of
Buddhism is the man from northern India
who became known as 'the Buddha'.

An auspicious birth

Siddartha Gautama was born in a family of
the *Kshatriya* caste, the warrior tradition.
His conception is reported to have been
accompanied by a vision, his mother
dreaming of a white elephant entering her
side. Signs in the heavens also attested to
the fact that he was to be a special child.
It was predicted that the child would be
either a great king or a holy ascetic. His
name, Siddartha, signified 'the one who
will attain the goal'.

He grew up as a prince and his father
tried to ensure that he had everything he
needed. He wanted Siddartha to grow up
with no contact with the unpleasantness
of life. He wanted nothing to disturb his
happiness. He was kept inside the palace,
isolated from anything tainted by either
suffering or death. He married a princess,
Yasodhara, and they had a son, Rahula.
Siddartha had everything he needed, but
he grew restless in his life of ease and
wanted to leave the palace to experience
life outside. When eventually he did, he
encountered the realities of life in a very
stark way.

The four signs

On his journey Siddartha saw what are
known as 'the four signs'. The first three
were an old man, a sick man, and a corpse.
He had never seen anything like this and

Meditation and mindfulness

Meditation[1] is an important aspect of Buddhist religious practice. It is thought to bring about spiritual growth and development. Its primary function, however, is to enable the practitioner to see things 'as they really are'. Mindfulness is a spiritual practice which leads the one who meditates to achieve this clarity of spiritual vision.

In their daily lives, human beings generally perform their tasks almost automatically, without giving much thought to the processes involved. Mindfulness or *sati* emphasizes the act of keeping something in mind with a strong awareness. It involves thorough observation, not just surface attention. The practitioner might eat a piece of fruit very, very slowly, being keenly aware of the tastes, texture, and colour of the food. Even the lifting up of an arm, or the act of walking slowly, will be observed and appreciated in minute detail, with the subject being mindful of every feeling and sensation. As a result, certain processes, which have perhaps always been a part of daily life, are experienced and noticed as if for the first time. This, in turn, encourages the ability of the mind to see things 'as they really are'.

was astounded when his charioteer said the same would happen to Siddartha. The final sign was an ascetic who, he discovered, was engaged in the quest to understand the transience of life and the significance of suffering. Siddartha immediately grasped that life was transitory. He wanted to base what was left of his life on a happiness that did not depend on his riches and status. He left his home and his security and began the path of renunciation and the search for the meaning of life. In the India of the time this was not an unusual decision to make. It is thought that he was twenty-nine years old.

Achieving enlightenment

Gautama sought out teachers who would lead him in meditative practices. But he felt he could learn only so much from them. He gathered others around him who would try to live out the ascetic life. For many years he adopted a rigorous lifestyle of prayer and fasting. His quest was for enlightenment, to see things as they really are. He wanted to achieve freedom from suffering which, he believed, stemmed from ignorance. Eventually, while meditating under the *bodhi* tree or 'enlightenment' tree, he did achieve that state of bliss and total understanding. This led to him being called 'the Buddha', a word which stems from the name of the tree of enlightenment.

On this path to enlightenment he had to fight off many demonic characters, particularly the being *Mara*, which is representative of the ensnarement of the world. He began to reject the extreme paths of asceticism he had practised in the past and tried to forge a 'middle way'. He was joined by disciples who wanted to learn from him and they travelled about northern India with him, preaching his message.

Gautama Buddha had attained a state in which he was able to feel no sense of self. This lack of concern for the self eliminated the fear of dying and of loss. He had begun to accept all of life's experiences as being impermanent. Attempting to keep hold of the impermanent could only lead to suffering. When human beings are not concerned with self-centredness, then they are in a state of not-self or *anatman*. This in turn can lead to *nirvana*, which is a feeling of bliss and enlightenment.

The *sangha*

After delivering his first sermon at the deer park outside Benares and being joined by his first followers, the Buddha before long established the *sangha*. This was a community of those who followed Gautama Buddha's teachings. He preached the middle path between the pursuit of pleasure and extreme bodily denial. The number of his followers increased quickly and the *sangha* grew in strength. To preach his message the Buddha travelled all around northern India. Those who through his teaching achieved enlightenment were known as *arhats*, since the title 'Buddha' could be held only by the one who had attained enlightenment by himself, rather than with the help of another. An *arhat* is one who is literally 'worthy'. The *arhat* has been set free from the cycle of birth and rebirth and has overcome desires which root human beings in selfishness and attachment.

The death of the Buddha

Prior to his death, the Buddha stipulated that none should succeed him since his teaching, known as the *dharma,* should be the guide. In his eightieth year the

Buddha died at the small town of Kusinara. Reverence for his memory and the honour in which he was destined to be held was apparent immediately in the way his remains were treated. After cremation his ashes were divided up and distributed.

The Buddha's cousin and close personal friend, Ananda, remained close to him to the end. His most influential disciple was Mahakasyapa. It is believed that it was Mahakasyapa who presided over the First Council held after the death of Buddha, at Rajagrha, the capital of Magadha. Here Ananda recited the Buddha's sayings and the material was checked for accuracy and learned by rote to be transmitted orally.

Monks lunch inside the Kyan Sit Thar Umin Theravada Buddhist monastery. The curry and rice dishes brought by the priests are placed on a wooden table and the monks take their meals sitting on the floor. The best curries are offered to the presiding monk who normally has a small table to himself.

Branches of Buddhism

Zen Buddhism is a mainly meditative approach. Tantra or *Vajrayana* is largely concerned with magic, including sexual magic. However, the dominant traditions of Buddhism are the *Theravada* and the *Mahayana*, each of them developing its own emphases and doctrinal stances. The former may be said to highlight the human Buddha, while the latter preaches a more transcendental Buddhism.

Theravada

Buddhism of the *Theravada* tradition is prevalent in Sri Lanka, Burma, Thailand, Laos, and Cambodia.

◆ *Theravada* Buddhists focus on monastic ideals and lifestyle and view the historical Buddha as an exemplar to follow, imitating his human existence.

◆ *Theravada* Buddhists believe Gautama Buddha was an ordinary man who attained extraordinary heights of enlightenment, but still remains only a human being and now guides the world through his teaching.

◆ To *Theravada* Buddhists the Buddha is not a divine or semi-divine being to whom people can still gain access. There are also others, they believe, who have attained and can attain Buddha-hood. Nonetheless, his images and person are still treated with enormous respect.

Mahayana

Mahayana Buddhism is influential in China, Japan, and Tibet, establishing itself as the dominant expression of the faith.

◆ *Mahayana* Buddhism consists of many schools of doctrine.

◆ Unlike *Theravada*, *Mahayana* is not a monastic tradition.

◆ The *Mahayana* path places great stress on the notion of 'Buddha-hood', a state that can be aspired to and which can be attained over many cycles of rebirth. A person moving close to such a state would be characterized by a compassionate nature and is known as a *bodhisattva*.

◆ *Mahayana* Buddhists also believe they follow a 'high' form of Buddhism which holds that there are heavenly beings or cosmic Buddhas who live in paradise and who help human beings with enlightenment. They live in cosmic realms known as the 'pure lands' and it is possible to be reborn there.

◆ *Mahayana* Buddhists believe the Buddha would not have abandoned the world, so he must in some way have an input into what is going on in it. Related to this view is the belief in the figure of the *bodhisattva,* a being on the path to full Buddha-hood, who serves others and is not limited only to the earth, but lives in heavenly realms also and can be active in the world in a god-like way.

In the West

There has been a massive increase in interest in Buddhism in the West. This is particularly true of Tibetan Buddhism and Zen Buddhism. In Britain, for example, the monastery of Kagyu Samye Ling in Scotland attracts numerous pilgrims and recruits to the monastic life, and most cities and many towns have Buddhist centres, teaching meditation and Buddhist philosophy. Buddhism can also be found on university campuses, offering courses and support to students. Western bookshops carry numerous titles that reflect a growing interest in Buddhism and Buddhist mysticism.

Buddhism for some may be just another lifestyle choice, a fast means to a shallow 'enlightenment' as it is divorced from its roots. Many, however, have found that Buddhism has offered them a meaningful and deep spiritual experience by which to explore existence.

Left: Buddhist monks circle golden Buddha statues at Fo Guang Shan Monastery in Kaohsiung, Taiwan.

A section of chapter 21 of the Medium-Length *Agon Sutra*, the earliest Buddhist canon, reflecting the fundamental teachings of the historical Buddha, dating from the Nara period (710–794 CE). This chapter is part of a set of *sutras* known as the *Zenko shuinkyo*.

Sacred Writings

The Buddha left nothing in writing and early Buddhist teaching was entirely in oral form, handed down from one generation to the next. A Buddhist teaching does not need to be written down but can be followed by listening, by reflection and by carrying it through in daily life. It was, therefore, as a vehicle of teaching, entirely suited for oral transmission.

An appreciation of *dharma* is important to any understanding of the nature and status of Buddhist scriptures.

◆ *Dharma* can be understood as the essential truth of the world.

◆ *Dharma* underlies everything.

◆ *Dharma* is also concerned with right action.

Thus, as human beings we should live our lives with *dharma* as our guide and the foundation of our daily lives and actions.

The three baskets

A few months after the death of the Buddha, the First Council was convened at Rajagrha. This was a gathering of perhaps some 500 followers who had each memorized his teachings. These teachings, which were recited communally, fell into two categories:

◆ the Buddha's general teachings, known as *sutras* (or *sutta* in the Pali language);

◆ teachings which had as their focus religious lifestyle and discipline, known as *vinaya*.

Gradually another category of scriptures emerged. These were known as

◆ *abhidhamma* or *abhidharma*, meaning 'further *dharma*'.

Taken together, the three categories of scripture were referred to as *tripitaka* in Sanskrit (*tipitaka* in Pali), meaning 'the three baskets'. Buddhist teaching is often expressed in both Sanskrit and Pali.

The *Theravada* (or Pali) canon

As Buddhism underwent its historical development, different schools of thought emerged and with them different versions of the canon of scriptures. In essence, three main canons exist today and these relate to the three most important traditions of Buddhism prevalent in the world today.

The *Theravada* canon, used by the branch of Buddhism of the same name, is also known as the Pali Canon, since it is written in the ancient Pali language. Pali is closely related to Sanskrit. Sanskrit is the ancient language of India and is the language in which much of Indian high culture is expressed. While Sanskrit is regarded as being a scholarly language, strongly associated with religious teaching, Pali was the vernacular of ordinary people at

the time of the Buddha. It is thought that the Buddha would have imparted his teachings in the ordinary language of his listeners.

The *Theravada* Buddhists believe the Pali canon was brought from northern India to Sri Lanka in the third century BCE. It is divided into three sections.

◆ The *Sutra Pitaka* consists of a series of dialogues. The term *sutra* means a 'thread'. These *sutras* are themselves divided into five sections, the *Nikayas*. The *sutras* primarily contain teaching. This teaching is not only about the Four Truths and the Eightfold path, but also about daily living.

◆ The *Vinaya Pitaka* contains more detailed exposition of the rules that should govern behaviour. It specifically focuses on monastic discipline, with emphasis on individual conduct in a section known as the *Pratimoksa*, and the conducting of ritual, discussed in detail in the *Skandhaka*.

◆ The *Abhidharma Pitaka* refers to a 'higher' or 'further' set of teaching on the *dharma*. This section is more analytical. It subjects the Buddha's teaching to a systematic treatment, taking a more psychological approach to understanding how different kinds of people can walk the Buddhist path.

The *Mahayana* scriptures

The *Mahayana* (also known as 'the Great Vehicle') branch of Buddhism has its own scriptural tradition. *Mahayana* scriptures began to emerge around the time of the

The Wheel of Dharma with two deer on the roof of Jokhang Temple, Lhasa, Tibet. The temple was built in the 7th century under King Songsten Gampo.

in Tibet into what is known as the *Vajrayana* canon. The scriptures in this canon consist of sections from the Pali canon, the *Mahayana* canon, and what is known as the *Tantras*. This is a magical aspect of Buddhism which uses sacred circles or *mandalas* and repeated *mantras*. Tantric Buddhism also teaches about the ritualistic use of sex to achieve spiritual attainment.

Core Beliefs

Buddhism is very diverse in its beliefs and practices. Buddhist groupings will differ in the emphasis they place on aspects of the Buddha's teaching. Buddhism is much more a way of life, a path to be followed, than a strict set of teachings. *Theravada* Buddhists place a greater stress on the ascetic lifestyle than do the *Mahayana* Buddhists who, in their own view, try to widen the focus of the Buddha's teachings to encompass a greater range of beliefs.

By far the vast majority of the world's 350 million Buddhists live in Asia, but there are, it is thought, about 1 million in the US and 3 million in Europe (including 200,000 Buddhists practising in the UK). Since many adherents practise Buddhism in private, definite figures are difficult to ascertain. In spite of its diversity, all Buddhists tend to follow certain core ideals and fundamentals.

The Four Noble Truths
The foundations of the Buddha's teachings are the Four Noble Truths (see table opposite). These reflect the goal of

birth of Christianity, between 100 BCE and 100 CE. They claimed to be the words of the Buddha himself, not commentaries on his teachings.

The *Mahayana Sutras* were not universally acknowledged as being the actual teachings of Buddha, but they did gather a lot of interest and many in the various schools of Buddhism in existence at the time did subscribe to them to one degree or another. As such they were influential. They were considered to be innovative and radical. They contain some of the material to be found in the Pali canon. It is thought that the *Mahayana* scriptures were translated into Sanskrit from the vernacular languages.

The *Vajrayana* canon
The *Mahayana* scriptures were expanded

The Four Noble Truths

The first of the truths is *dukkha*, the truth about suffering.	This accepts that suffering is an inescapable part of life. It leads to unhappiness and dissatisfaction. A wide-ranging term, *dukkha* can describe an unfortunate state of affairs such as sickness, death or misfortune or the unhappiness felt when one is separated from that which normally causes pleasure.
The second truth, *samudya*, teaches that suffering arises from a source and that source is craving and thirst or *tanh*.	It equates with desire and is the driving force of the dissatisfaction which is allied to suffering.
The third truth assures us that there is the possibility of cessation or *nirodha* from suffering.	This teaches that when craving is dispensed with, suffering comes to an end and *nirvana* can be attained.
The fourth truth explains that the path to this cessation, *magga*, is the Eightfold Path, also known as the 'Middle Way'.	It is so called because it attempts to steer a medial path between a life which is too indulgent and one which involves too much asceticism.

Buddhism in ending the cycle of suffering and rebirth.

Dukkha
Dukkha refers to any suffering, either physical or mental. It recognizes that no permanence is possible in this life. Accepting this should lead to an end of craving and desire, since the human being will realize that nothing can last forever anyway. The better way is to let go of desire.

The Eightfold Path
The Eightfold Path describes the way to the end of suffering. The eight aspects of the path are all related to each other.

◆ Right understanding is concerned with seeing things as they really are, in their state of impermanence, futility and decay.

◆ Right thought encourages the mind to think differently. The mind should develop the qualities of compassion, love, kindness and reverence towards all living beings. Selfish desires need to be rejected. This path is concerned with motivation.

◆ Right speech dispenses with the need to lie, slander, or use abusive language.

◆ Right action leads to non-violence and respect for all life. It also deals with the area of sexual conduct.

The three defining marks of existence

Within *dharma* – the second of the Three Refuges chanted by Buddhists throughout the world – lie a further three foundational teachings of the Buddhist path.[2]

Dharma or *dhamma* is understood to be truth. It is the very law of nature itself, the reason why everything is as it is. It encompasses three views of life which are known as the three *signata* or defining marks of existence.

◆ The first is the quality known as *anicca*. This refers to the impermanence of all things in life. Nothing ever remains exactly the same, but everything is in a constant process of change.

◆ The second quality, *dukkha*, consists of everything that has its roots in dissatisfaction with human existence and knowing it is devoid of ultimate meaning. The most common explanation of *dukkha* is suffering, but its full meaning is not limited to physical or emotional distress. Dissatisfaction with all that life has to offer leads to a particular kind of suffering which springs from the acceptance that life can never give any fulfilment.

◆ *Anatta*, the third defining mark of existence, is the understanding that impermanence is a fundamental characteristic of what it means to be a human. It is often translated as meaning 'no-soul'. It holds that the human body is subject to the same process of impermanence as anything else. The human being has no ultimate control over his or her body since the bodily processes take their own course irrespective of what the human being tries to do. Effectively, death and decay are inevitable.

◆ Right livelihood requires the follower to ensure that he or she engages in a job or profession which is not harmful to others. It stresses the need for integrity in whatever the disciple does.

◆ Right effort emphasizes the need to think about what the disciple says and does in daily life. It also deals with the issue of over-indulgence or under-indulgence and encourages temperance and moderation.

◆ Right awareness, also known as 'mindfulness', expects the follower of the path to be alert and awake in life. It teaches the disciple that he or she must think about the issues of life and make wise choices. This path encourages meditation.

◆ Right concentration is again concerned with meditation. It leads to a detachment from the world. The disciple who meditates also becomes at peace. Meditation can cause the disciple to progress through states known as *jhanas*. Each state brings an increased sense of happiness.

The Five Precepts

Buddhists believe that the law of *karma* or 'action' means that living beings are trapped in a cycle of birth and rebirth. Each action has a consequence. Buddhist ethics are encapsulated in the Five Precepts:

I undertake the precept to abstain from killing living beings.
I undertake the precept to abstain from taking what is not given.
I undertake the precept to abstain from sexual misconduct.
I undertake the precept to abstain from false speech.
I undertake the precept to abstain from alcohol and drugs.

The Three Jewels

A Buddhist will confess his or her adherence to the path by reciting the Three Refuges, also known as the 'Three Jewels' or 'Three Gems'.

I go to the Buddha for refuge.
I go to the Dharma for refuge.
I go to the Sangha for refuge.

Buddhists believe that, by getting rid of the cravings and delusions which lead to the cycle of rebirth, they can attain the state of *nirvana*. They differ as to whether this can take place in one's own lifetime or takes place in another

The Yonghe Temple in Beijing, China, is also known as the Lama Temple. It is one of the largest Tibetan monasteries.

realm. *Nirvana* is a highly desired state of freedom from the birth–rebirth drama. It is defined as pure and ineffable bliss.

Worship and Festivals

The one constant feature in the many styles of Buddhist worship is the prevalence of the image of the Buddha. He is not always regarded as a god figure, although in practice he is sometimes treated that way.

Buddhist temples

In a typical temple one will find shrine rooms where an image of the Buddha is revered and where offerings of flowers and food may be placed before it. In *Mahayana* Buddhism some images of the *bodhisattvas* will be displayed, particularly Amida or Avalokitesvara. In *Theravada* Buddhism the image is the Buddha's. Lotus buds, symbols of purity, and incense lights will usually adorn the images.

Within the grounds of temples and in various places in the open air will be found relic mounds or *stupas*. Originally these were built over the cremated remains of a king or a spiritual teacher; today they usually contain a relic of a Buddhist holy person. Shrine rooms within temples may contain miniature versions of a *stupa*. A temple will also have living quarters for the monks and nuns. Next to those is normally a bo or bodhi tree, which represents the tree under which Gautama Buddha found enlightenment. Meditation rooms are also important within Buddhist temples, particularly in the *Zen* tradition.

Inside a temple worshippers will remove their shoes as a mark of respect. Often Buddhists will prostrate themselves while remembering the 'Three Jewels' or 'Three Refuges'. Prostrations are a sign of self-surrender and humility. They may bring offerings of food and flowers, and offer prayers and devotion according to their faith position within Buddhism.

Worship at home

Buddhists can worship individually or corporately. A devout Buddhist may have a place in the home which has an image of the Buddha where prayers can be offered and where the believer can engage in meditation. In both individual and corporate worship, prayer beads can be used to keep count of either prayers or prostrations, and prayer wheels may be spun to symbolize continuous prayer. Prayer wheels may be adorned with the phrase '*Om mani padme hum*', which translates as 'Hail, jewel in the lotus bud' and is regarded as a powerful *mantra*.

Funeral rites

Generally, Buddhists cremate their dead, although in Tibet the custom is usually to leave the body exposed to nature, owing to the scarcity of wood. Monks use funerals as occasions on which they can remind worshippers and mourners of the impermanence of life. The family of the deceased will give offerings to the monks, and the merit accrued by this deed will be given to the deceased to assist his or her rebirth.

Rites of passage

Initiation is an important feature of life in Buddhism, particularly within the monastic tradition. Young boys may be initiated into the monastic life for a short period of time to symbolize their desire to live by the right path. Some may choose to stay for a much longer time or choose the monastic path as their way of life.

Birth is not treated with the same degree of ritual celebration as in other societies and birth celebrations tend to be of a secular nature or according to local tradition. Similarly, the marriage ceremony is generally considered a secular institution. Ceremonies are simple. In some societies astrological charts are eagerly consulted to ascertain whether the bride and groom may be compatible.

Festivals

Buddhist countries all tend to adhere to a

Monks unfurl a huge *thangka* painting on the slope of a hill at Monlam, the Great Prayer Festival, Labrang Tashikyil Monastery, Tibet.

different calendar and each has developed its own distinct festivals. *Mahayana* Buddhists will also celebrate special days for the various *bodhisattvas* and cosmic Buddhas.

Especially during festivals Buddhists may involve themselves in community worship. During *Wesak*, which is held at the full moon in May, Buddhists celebrate the birth, enlightenment, and death of the Buddha. This takes place in the temple, where devotion is offered. *Wesak* is a time for giving presents and for decorating the home and temples.

Pilgrimage is an important part of Buddhist practice, although it is not a requisite of leading a good life. Giant statues of the Buddha can be found dotted throughout South-East Asia and other parts of the East. The extensive complex at Borobudur near Yogyakarta in Java, abandoned for centuries and overgrown but now a World Heritage Site, is particularly magnificent. Some sites connected with the Buddha serve as a focal point for festivals or pilgrimage and prayer.

Family and Society

Because the monastic tradition is so strong within Buddhism, it is easy to make the mistake of viewing it as primarily a religious path which can only be followed by monks, or *bhikkus*, and nuns, also called *bhikkunis*. However, it would be a particularly unhelpful faith if it could not be accessed and followed by ordinary people in their daily lives.

Lay participation
The story goes that the Buddha, questioned by Vacchagotta the Wanderer about the involvement of laymen and laywomen in following the Buddha's teaching, replied that there were many hundreds who listened to him and were able to gain a high degree of spiritual insight.

Although monks and nuns are able to detach themselves from the cares and responsibilities of the world, lay people find it harder to do so. However, it is recognized that many in monastic orders might, in fact, be living self-indulgent lives while those who are immersed in the world and in family matters may be leading lives of great self-sacrifice. Generally it is acknowledged that monks, nuns, laymen, and laywomen are all inter-related in some way and each has a role to play in the whole societal order. The laity provide monks and nuns with food and alms and are in turn taught by them.

Family relations
In Buddhism the concept of family is important. Buddha himself regarded parents as being worthy of respect from their children because they discharge a sacred duty of care and teaching. Children should look after parents in their old age. Parents are expected to educate children well, protect them from evil choices, and teach them to spend their time profitably. Wives and husbands are told that they should be respectful, one to another, and love each other. They complement each other and may have different duties. The wife looks after the house and makes it into

a place of hospitality. The husband treats the wife with respect and gives her the material things she needs to make the home a prosperous place in all respects.

In a religion characterized by such emphasis on right action and right thought, it is not surprising that general members of society are expected to treat each other with care and respect, each working for the other's welfare. Buddhist teaching should, in a Buddhist society, permeate all of the institutions of the state. Buddhism should not be seen as concerned only with high philosophical ideals, but with the happiness of society. Therefore, the Buddhist view of society is both holistic and balanced. Good economic wellbeing is regarded as essential for happiness and peace, but without peace and harmony it is useless.

Contemporary Issues

In its traditional heartlands in Asia, Buddhism has suffered from changing political regimes which have marginalized it and from Communism and other political philosophies that have tried to eliminate its influence or persecute its adherents. In many societies there have been demands for increased lay involvement and this has challenged the monastic status quo.

The role of women
Historical Buddhism has demonstrated an ambivalent attitude towards the position of women, viewing them both as a distraction and as being able to achieve spiritual enlightenment alongside men, although nuns had a lower status than monks. In early Buddhism, rich women were important benefactors of the faith.

Contemporary Buddhists who try to understand the position of women within Buddhism are increasingly looking to early Buddhism for answers to establish more equal structures. Nevertheless, Buddhist women continually have to deal with ambiguous attitudes in Buddhist history and texts. The stratification of the *sangha* means that senior nuns are ranked below junior monks.

Three monks at Sera Monastery, Lhasa, Tibet.

Reading guide to Buddhism

Conze, Edward, *Buddhism: Its Essence and Development*, Bruno Cassirer, Oxford, 1957 edn.

Conze, Edward, *A Short History of Buddhism*, Unwin Paperbacks, London, 1982 edn.

Cush, Denise, *Buddhism*, Hodder & Stoughton, 1998 edn.

Gethin, Rupert, *The Foundations of Buddhism*, Oxford Paperbacks, Oxford University Press, 1998.

Harris, Elizabeth J., *What Buddhists Believe*, Oneworld, Oxford, 2001 edn.

Harvey, Peter, *An Introduction to Buddhism: Teachings, History and Practices*, Cambridge University Press, Cambridge, 1990.

Keown, Damien, *Buddhism,* Oxford University Press, 1996.

Klostermaier, Klaus, K., *Buddhism: A Short Introduction*, Oneworld, Oxford, 2002 edn.

Lopez, Donald S., *Buddhism: An Introduction and Guide*, Allen Lane, Penguin Press, London, 2001.

Robinson, Richard H., *The Buddhist Religion: An Historical Introduction*, Dickenson Publishing Company, Inc, Belmont, California, 1970.

Subhuti, Dharmachari, *Bringing Buddhism to the West: A Life of Sangharakshita*, Windhorse Publications, Birmingham, 1995.

Within *Theravada* Buddhism there are numerous lay movements for women in which many are extremely active. Women tend to enjoy a higher status within *Mahayana* Buddhism, which is less influenced by monasticism.

Buddhism in the West

One of the most significant developments within Buddhism in modern times has been its popularity in the West. The absence of a deity within Buddhism makes it acceptable as a spiritual philosophy which can instil both ethics and discipline into daily life. As an undogmatic faith system it appeals to an age which is comfortable with constructing its own religious paths from a variety of sources. The interest in Buddhism could be seen as a response to increased secularization by those who cannot find answers to their spiritual searching in traditional church life. Buddhist concepts of rebirth and of integration into an organic whole make more sense to a society which sees itself as ecologically sensitive, as does the Buddhist notion of non-violence and care for all living things.

Tibetan Buddhism, as a result of the Chinese invasion of 1959, has been able through its diaspora to disseminate Buddhist teaching all over the world. Many Westerners travel to Buddhist countries to experience Buddhist spirituality and explore it as a viable path for life. European intellectual interest in Buddhism dates from the mid-eighteenth century, but this was amplified in the nineteenth century with an explosion of interest as a result of travel into Buddhist lands and the translation of Buddhist texts into European languages.

Confucianism

History and Development

The origins of Confucianism can be traced back to the ancient Shang dynasty (1766–1122 BCE) which encouraged and fostered spirituality. The Shang believed in a spirit world that could be contacted and they practised divination, by which the spirits could be consulted and their wishes discerned.

Before the fall of the Han Dynasty (206 BCE–220 CE), classical Confucianism had enjoyed the role of state ideology. However, with the fall of the dynasty came Confucianism's decline. The disorder which came to society as the Han Dynasty moved towards a close cast a shadow also over the status of Confucianism as a philosophy of good government.

As it began to stagnate, elements of Taoism were introduced to Confucianism by scholars of the Wei-Jin Dynasties (220 CE–420 CE). With the ascendancy of Buddhism, Confucianism began to face serious competition from both Buddhism and Taoism. However, during the Sui and Tang Dynasties (581 CE–907 CE), Confucianism began to regain some of its status. Confucian scholars gained increasing influence in government and administration and the scholar Han Yu (768 CE–824 CE) played a major role in reviving Confucian fortunes. He opposed Buddhism and paved the way for a more confident Confucianism to find ways to learn from both Buddhism and Taoism, yet retain its own distinctive character. As scholars began to rediscover the ancient texts of the classical Confucian period, a significant revival of interest in Confucian philosophy occurred. It was out of this that Neo-Confucianism grew in the tenth century CE.

Size Confucianism is counted among the Chinese traditional religions, which together may number about 394 million adherents. Estimates of purely Confucian adherents indicate a figure of about 6 million.

Founder Confucius (c. 552–479 BCE) is the traditional Western spelling of the name K'ung fu-tzu (meaning something like 'wise master K'ung').

Location Originating in China in the sixth century BCE, Confucianism spread outwards to Vietnam, Korea, Japan, and Singapore.

Statue of Confucius, from Ho Chi Minh City, Vietnam.

Founder and Significant Figures

The founder of Confucianism is in modern Chinese often called 'Kong Zi'. In the West his name has many spellings. His Latinized name, Confucius, is attributed to Jesuit missionaries who made their way into China in the seventeenth century.

The great teacher

The date of Confucius's birth is uncertain, but is generally given as 552 or 551 BCE. Born in the province of Shantung (now Shandung) in the state of Lu, he grew up as an educated young man in spite of his humble beginnings. He entered into what were basically administrative positions, eventually working for the government. As he worked in administration, he was able to see at first hand the injustice and oppression going on around him. He developed his ethical and religious teaching in this context, aware that human beings had become cynical by the actions of those above him and recognizing that the state needed to be reformed. During his life he gathered a number of followers around him. He died in 479 BCE. In his home town of Qufu a complex of buildings associated with him is now listed as a UNESCO World Heritage Site (China's second largest historical building complex after the Forbidden City).

The way of Confucius

Two principles, above all, define Confucianism.[1] Both are vital in establishing harmonious human relationships, which can be built on firm foundations.

- *Jen* is understood as kindness. It encompasses the notion of unconditional love and represents a desire for the highest good for all.

- *Li* is interpreted as propriety. The concept includes duty, righteousness, and honesty and carries with it the sense of correct conduct and the exercise of justice and fairness. Its association with *jen* comes about because *jen* without *li* may be nothing more than sentimentality. *Jen* may encourage mercy, but justice is also important in establishing a fair and proper society.

An important quality to acquire is *chih* or wisdom. This enables the practitioner of *jen* and *li* to discern between good and bad behaviour and understand how to apply *li*.

Developing the individual

Carrying on the moral teaching of Confucius and building on it, Meng-tzu or Mencius (372–289 BCE) was another important figure in Confucianism. He did not concentrate so much on the importance of the state, but rather on the individual within it. Human beings were not simply products of society, but needed the freedom to grow and develop morally so that they could contribute to society. If the individual were allowed to attain his or her potential, then the state would automatically benefit.

Society's role

Another great Confucian teacher, Hsün-tzu (about 312–230 BCE), also known as Xun Zi, taught that it was the role of society to nurture the individual. Society could not pass this responsibility on to gods and spirits. Having said that, he taught that ritual action had a prime role in transforming the human being.

Branches of Confucianism

Chu Hsi (1130–1200), also known as Zhu Xi, exercised a strong influence over the development of Neo-Confucianism. As an author and a teacher, his major role was in interpreting classical Confucian doctrine for a new era. He emphasized that the self must be known thoroughly so that spiritual progress can take place. This self-knowing took place gradually, over time. The *ultimate* can be known by the human being. This *ultimate* is not to be understood as a personal God, but rather as the impersonal ultimate life force of the universe, the ground of all being.

Wang Yang-ming (1472–1529) is often compared with Chu Hsi because of his influence on Neo-Confucianism. However, he disagreed with Chu Hsi on many areas of doctrine and philosophy, regarding the direction of Chu Hsi's teaching as overcomplicated.

Wang Yang-ming had a varied life. He was a government official for some time, then joined the army only to fall from grace because he had offended a powerful official. He spent a great deal of time in study and became one of Neo-Confucianism's most influential philosophers and reinterpreters of doctrine.

The influence of Confucianism can be found in Korea, Vietnam, Japan, and Singapore. In Singapore the government has viewed Confucian values as key to establishing a stable society, which has resulted in economic success, although some in the nation have criticized the use of such values as a means to uphold what they see as an authoritarian style of society. In Korea, Vietnam, and Japan those in authority

The Chinese philosopher, Mencius (c. 372–289 BCE), is dressed in his official cap and robes.

have traditionally seen Confucianism as a model for good government and each of these nations has adapted its teachings to its own particular set of circumstances. In these societies too, elements of the population view Confucianism as a system that can be used to promote authoritarianism ahead of freedom.

Sacred Writings

The teachings of Confucius were set out as records of conversations with his disciples. This collection is known as the *Analects of Confucius*.

The other major scriptures of Confucianism, known as the *Five Classics*, consist of:

- *I-Ching*, also known as the *Book of Changes*, which describes rites of divination and also deals with philosophical issues;

- *Shang Shu*, a collection of historical documents made up of the speeches of kings and important political figures, which also deals with principles of government;

- *Shijing*, made up of poems and songs;

- the *Classic of Rites*, setting out the rituals needed for various ceremonies such as marriage, funerals and state or community occasions, and incorporating the *Book of Rites*, the *Liji*, which sets out teaching on education and philosophy;

- *Chunqiu*, a set of annals which records the affairs of the state of Lu.

Traditionally, all of the classics have been attributed to Confucius, although modern scholarship dismisses this idea. The writings associated with Confucianism are regarded as being works of philosophy as much as works of religious teaching and merit.

Core Beliefs

The core of Confucian belief is the fundamental goodness of humanity, even in the midst of great cruelty and injustice. The fostering of good human relationships is paramount in achieving harmony and justice. Humanity is regarded as a family within which these relationships must be developed and good relationships within families are themselves models for good relationships in society as a whole. Inner conversion produces outward good behaviour and good example is crucial in teaching good behaviour and inner rectitude.

Confucius urged his disciples to become model citizens, or *chung-tzu*, and to teach through their own actions the principles of a moral life. If the rulers of society themselves became *chung-tzu*, then harmony based on morality and religion would filter and permeate through society as a whole. Confucius himself is remembered as a prime example of this model human being.

The principle of harmony

Confucius believed that religious rites were useful means to demonstrate in a visual way the importance of harmony. He placed great emphasis on the correct carrying out of rites and rituals and the use of music and poetry. When this happened, harmony occurred. This harmony would also emerge when people behaved properly towards each other in family and society. Over time, this harmony would affect hearts and minds. He described this principle of harmony as *li*. The formation of *li* in the heart and mind of the human being was known as *yi*.

When the human being is acting in a truly humane way towards others, he or she is said to be exercising the quality of *ren*. This is the overwhelming characteristic of the *chung-tzu*. The elders in any society have a vital role in teaching the younger members and it is incumbent on the elders to encourage *chung-tzu*. Human beings should not be shaped by outward forces but by the moral force within. This will express itself in right living, in harmony, in forgiveness and ultimately in a just and peaceful society.

The teaching of Confucius, then, forms the basis for a political as well as a religious philosophy. He emphasized the importance of good relationships between rulers and their people. Rulers must attain to the highest moral standards so that they serve as a model to the people.

A large barrel is placed under a pagoda. This pagoda is in the Temple of Literature, which was founded in 1070 as a Confucian temple. Vietnam's first university was established within the temple in 1076.

Performers are pictured at the National Stadium, or Birds' Nest, in Beijing during the opening ceremony of the 2008 Olympic Games. The 29th Olympic Games opened with a spectacular fireworks display.

Worship and Festivals

Confucianism does not worship a deity, although at times believers have attributed divine status to Confucius. Confucius himself did worship divine heavenly beings. He offered sacrifices to them and believed strongly in the importance of religious ritual. In 1906, the Chinese authorities attempted to name Confucianism as the state religion, which would have meant bestowing a divine status on Confucius. The attempt did not succeed. By contrast, Confucianism was severely repressed during the period when Mao Zedong (1893–1976) was in control. The Communist Party subjected many adherents to persecution.

Although Confucius is not revered as a god, he is respected as one who embodies morality. In Confucianism, the idea of heaven is viewed in different ways. It can be understood as a representation of the highest possible moral imperative. When heaven and earth meet in just rule then harmony and peace result.

Confucian ritual

Family rituals such as coming of age ceremonies, marriage, and funerals are all important parts of Confucianism. Familial ancestors continue to be respected and remembered in ritual. Although Confucius is not regarded as divine, the rituals which surround the reverence offered to him are religious in character. Confucius himself enacted rituals to divine beings and ancestors, so his followers see nothing wrong in offering similar rituals of respect to him. Hymns can be sung in his honour and his memory is held as sacred.

Reading guide to Confucianism

Bahm, Archie J., *The Heart of Confucius: Interpretation of Genuine Living and Great Wisdom*, Asian Humanities Press, Berkeley, USA, 1992 edn.

Billington, Ray, *Understanding Eastern Philosophy*, Routledge, London and New York, 1999 edn.

Creel, Herrlee G., *What Is Taoism and Other Studies in Chinese Cultural History*, University of Chicago Press, Chicago and London, 1982 edn.

McNaughton, William, ed., *The Confucian Vision*, Ann Arbor Paperbacks, University of Michigan Press, 1974.

Taylor, Rodney L., *The Confucian Way of Contemplation*, University of South Carolina Press, 1988.

Family and Society

Relationships are important in Confucianism and proper order in society is dependent on order in the family and in the life of the individual. One result of this emphasis on relationships is that these become rigidly fixed and applied. Historically, Chinese society has been distinctly patriarchal, with men taking the most important roles. With a changing society in China, where many women have broken away from their traditional roles, relationships within the family can often be much more equal.

Confucianism places great importance on societal harmony and good government. Where the rulers are ruling justly, it is believed that society will prosper. People must treat others as they would want to be treated, and while there is a sense of mutual subordination in Confucianism, there is still a great deal of respect offered to the elders in society and to authority. As a result, authoritarianism may be viewed as an acceptable form of government, as long as it results in a just and harmonious society and nation.

Contemporary Issues

Following the death of Mao Zedong in 1976, Confucianism began to prosper again. Confucian ideals had remained strongly ingrained in the national consciousness. As a result of the Communist rule of mainland China, Confucianism tended to gain greater influence in Taiwan, but its influence can still be discerned in general Chinese family life and relationships and it tends to be the dominant philosophy with regard to how family should function. Many scholars think that as China enters an unprecedented period of change and modernization, Confucianism may prove to be a guiding principle once more for the nation.

The opening ceremony of the 2008 Olympic Games in Beijing provided contemporary China with the ideal platform to show the importance of Confucius to Chinese society in modern times. Dancers and actors dressed up as Confucian scholars to put on a remarkable display in which they chanted Confucian sayings and extolled Confucian values. Confucianism is also promoted through films and television programmes about his life and teachings. Yu Dan's book, *Notes on the Analects of Confucius*, has been a publishing phenomenon in China, selling millions of copies. A professor at Beijing Normal University, Yu Dan also presented a series on the *Analects* on China Central Television.

11

Taoism

History and Development

Taoism, also known as Daoism, is one of the ancient religions of China. It emerged as a philosophical system about a century after the death of Confucius in 479 BCE and developed into both a system of philosophy and a religious system.

Size Taoism is counted amongst the grouping known as Chinese traditional religions. Estimates for purely Taoist practice stand at about 2.5 million.

Founder The sacred text of Taoism, the *Tao Te Ching*, is credited to Lao-tzu, but his existence is far from certain.

Location Originating in China, probably between the sixth and the fourth centuries BCE, and still concentrated here, the Taoist religion has gained some Western adherents through interest in its principal text, the *Tao Te Ching*.

Its date of origin is disputed and speculation ranges from the sixth century BCE to the fourth century BCE or even later.

The path or the way

Taoism is traditionally a contemplative path which dwells on inner discipline. The original meaning of *Tao* is a way, a road, or a path. It still has that meaning in Chinese today: a physical path. Within the religious system of Taoism, this path is taken to be spiritual. However, it is more than a path. It is also an immanent power within the universe. It is present everywhere, but is hidden from our eyes and can only be discerned through spiritual insight. It is concerned with the correct way in which life should be lived.

The *Tao* in Chinese thought

Confucius (c. 552–479 BCE) had striven to instil into the state principles of correct behaviour, both inward and outward. He was concerned with correct government.

When Confucius spoke of *Tao*, he imbued it with a meaning that was associated with rules and regulations. Following these will lead to a well ordered society. That the concept of the *tao* was also a focus of the teaching of Confucius is a reminder that the idea itself is not exclusive to what is normally accepted as classical Taoism, but is a feature of many schools of Chinese thought.

The concept of *Tao* promulgated by the reputed founder of Taoist philosophy, Lao-tzu, followed a very different set of principles. The legend, and it can be called no more than a legend because of the absence of any corroborating proof, claims that Lao-tzu and Confucius actually met each other and held conversations with each other about the *Tao*. What *is* known is that the book which Lao-tzu is credited with having written, the *Tao Te Ching*, is concerned not with earthly power and influence, nor with the evolution of society, but rather with the spiritual development of the individual. Inner harmony is its message.

The structures of society are man-made, they are human constructs. The *Tao*, according to the *Tao Te Ching*, is concerned with nature itself and with nature shaping the individual person; and this nature is imbued with the power of the *Tao*. The influence of the *Tao* on the individual may even be at odds with what is happening in society and may be counter-cultural, leading the individual to transcend society and societal expectations and demands.

Taoism quickly took on strongly metaphysical overtones, in contrast with the Confucian focus on the societal and the political.

Taoism and spiritual development

Later Taoism incorporated into itself elements of alchemy, the focus being the inner transformation of the human being. Both meditation and yoga were used to produce an internal awareness of immortality and oneness with all things. Taoism placed great emphasis on knowing through intuition and contemplation.

Taoism and Confucianism existed for

many centuries in mutual discussion and debate. The rise of Buddhism had a significant impact on both paths, with Taoism setting up monastic institutions after its example and putting down in writing its own texts. Confucianism engaged philosophically with Buddhism and this interaction affected its own evolution. The era of the Ming dynasty (1369–1644 CE) saw a certain harmonization of the thought systems of the three great faiths.

Founder and Significant Figures

The two figures most widely acknowledged as the founding fathers of the Taoist religion stand in sharp contrast to one another.

Lao-tzu

The very existence of Lao-tzu is far from certain. His first biographer, in the first century BCE, complained there was so little known about him it was impossible to write anything concrete. It is thought that he was from the village of Chu Jen, known today

Above: A Song dynasty statue of Lao-tzu in Quanzhou. Lao-tzu was the Chinese master philosopher and father of Taoism.

Previous page: Illustration of a procession to a Taoist wedding in China, c. 1820–39.

as Luyi and now a centre of pilgrimage for those wishing to see his birthplace – but he is more elusive than William Shakespeare, whose contribution to certain plays is disputed by experts.

His real name may have been Li Tan, the name Lao-tzu being a title of respect meaning 'Old Master' or 'Venerable Master'. He was, it is claimed, a court archivist for the state of Chou. The authorship of the key text, *Tao Te Ching*, is attributed to him, yet it is impossible to state whether he wrote it. The account given of its authorship is that shortly before his death an innkeeper or a sentry, aware that a stranger of great wisdom was in town, asked him to write down his thoughts and philosophy: he at that point wrote the *Tao*.

Lao-tzu, philosopher and central figure of Taoism, c. 6th century BCE.

Although the figure of Lao-tzu exists in legend, scholars believe the *Tao Te Ching* was written in around the fourth century BCE and, rather than being written by one figure, is a compilation of wisdom about the *Tao* and the *Te* gathered over many centuries and eventually edited into one volume.

Chuang-tzu

A disciple of Lao-tzu, known as Chuang-tzu (c. 369–286 BCE), is thought to have written another influential book about the *Tao*, known as the *Chuang-tzu*. It is commonly thought that this is an expansion of Lao-tzu's own philosophy, but some scholars see it as quite different from the *Tao Te Ching* in its approach. The *Chuang-tzu* gets its message across through humour and anecdote and only occasionally uses the *Tao Te Ching* as source material. It develops the concept of the *Tao* into other dimensions, with Chuang-tzu himself subverting convention through his stories and illustrations. It retains similarity with the *Tao Te Ching* in the way in which it emphasizes the importance of the individual and nature. Mystical union with nature brings happiness and freedom.

Branches of Taoism

As Taoism became more established it diversified into many different expressions. It exists both as a philosophy and as a religious and ritual practice.

◆ During the third to sixth centuries CE *non-Taoism* emerged out of philosophical Taoism as a religion with rites and activities. It also brought poetry and art into the religious mix.

◆ The beginning of Taoism as a religious path is often associated with the *Heavenly Masters* sect, founded in the second century CE. Supposedly based on supernatural revelation from Lao-tzu himself, the sect began to formalize Taoist philosophy into religious action in an attempt to create a better society. The sect is still popular in southern China. It has its headquarters in Taiwan.

◆ The *Perfect Truth* sect places strong emphasis on asceticism and abstinence and is dedicated to meditation.

The development of Taoism has been strongly influenced by both Confucianism and Buddhism. The religious thinker Lin Chao-en (1517–98) sought to bring about greater harmony between these three faiths by emphasizing the points of unity they shared. The result has been that, even in modern-day China, it is not uncommon for religious believers to blend elements from all three religions together in their own faith.

Sacred Writings

The principal text of classical Taoism is the *Tao Te Ching*. Tradition states that it was written by Lao-tzu in the sixth century BCE. The title means 'The Way and its power'. The book defines what *Tao* is, then explores this concept.

◆ The *Tao Te Ching* is written in a sparse, terse style which may owe something to its oral origins. Short, pithy sayings are grouped together in the text.

◆ It does not follow one single argument right through. Rather, it is a collection of

The *Tao Te Ching*

The *Tao Te Ching* is one of the most important and influential books of Chinese literature.[1] The title *ching* is honorary and is given to books that are regarded as being classic. The *Tao* itself is essentially the ground of all being. The term *tao* is found throughout Chinese philosophy, meaning a road or a path. From this interpretation came the understanding that the *Tao* primarily had to do with a sense of right conduct or action. In Confucianism it is a way of living – a principle by which the individual should live. In Taoism, the notion of *Tao* takes on a deeper meaning: a substance from which everything else that exists derives its existence. It is the totality of all being and the reality which sustains the universe. Within Taoism, the *Tao* is a metaphysical concept rather than a moral path.

◆ The *Tao* is unknowable and can only be discerned because of the forces which flow from it. It is an underlying reality, the consequences of which may be understood by the human mind, but whose own essential reality cannot be grasped or appraised.

◆ The *Tao* is the source of the *ch'i,* the breath of life-force from which the universe was formed.

◆ It is the source of *yin* and *yang,* the twin principles that represent the polar opposites which regulate all of existence.

◆ The manifestation of the *Tao* is known as the *Te*. It is the manifestation of the power of the *Tao* in the world.

◆ The *Tao* is expressed through existence being true to its own nature. When something follows its nature, this is the *Te* expressing the integrity of the *Tao*.

The *Tao Te Ching* consists of 5,000 pictograms in eighty-one chapters. It is a short text and is meant to be read in a meditative style. It is made up of spiritual teaching, wisdom, observations about the natural order of things, and mystical sayings.

sayings which are designed to instigate thought and contemplation.

◆ It is about 5,000 pictograms long and many of its statements are cryptic, raising more questions than they answer.

◆ Its message is that human beings must or should seek reunion with the nature from which they have become divorced.

◆ The Tao is presented as having pre-existence before creation, the foundational source of all things.

◆ It speaks of a form of living, or an attitude of living, known as *wu-wei*. This is best described as 'non-action', not in the sense of inaction, but of a lack of fixation on the need for action.

◆ It speaks of 'being', of living in the power of nature without feeling the need to react unnecessarily to everything. It emphasizes withdrawal from the world rather than attachment to it.

Core Beliefs

For Taoists, salvation is there for the whole person, the body as well as the soul. There are three 'life principles' which Taoists believe in:

◆ *qi* is breath;

◆ *jing* is the essential seed of life (such as that found in sperm);

◆ *shen* is spirit.

Each of these three principles is present both in the individual human and at the same time in the whole of creation.

Immortality is a key feature of Taoist belief. Healing and wholeness are important and take place through sacred breathing exercises and meditation. In ancient times a kind of alchemy which involved the ingestion of dangerous substances was practised. These substances would help preserve the body after death, but they also hastened death. Therefore, Taoists practise a form of 'inner alchemy' that enables interior spiritual transformation to occur, which in turn enables immortality.

Worship and Festivals

As the Taoist religion took hold in daily life, religious rituals were established. Believers were told how to lead fulfilled and happy lives and the actions of this life were linked to happiness in an afterlife. Taoism developed the features of a salvific religion, looking on the human being as having fallen and as being in need of renewal through religious practice.

Heroes, gods, semi-magic

Taoism has, over time, developed a belief in a number of different spiritual beings, god figures and celestial heroic characters, including Lao-tzu. Taoism even developed a trinity of gods, each god of the trinity having a different aspect and role. At festivals around the New Year prayers are made to the stove god, an important figure in Taoism. People burn pieces of paper which have prayers written on them and which are given as a sacrificial offering.

Taoism has its own system of priests and rituals. Priests carry out both blessings and exorcisms. Priests also have an important role in semi-magical practices which involve astrology, spiritualism, and necromancy.

Festivals

The Taoist year is punctuated at regular intervals with colourful festivals. Taoists believe food can contain either positive or negative energy and each festival will have its own particular focus. Dumplings or special cakes will often be made. There are street parades, during which firecrackers are let off, floats are decorated with flowers, and the symbols of the lion and the dragon are plentiful. People dress up in colourful costumes, puppet shows are put on, and large masked models are made.

The winter solstice is the occasion for a major festival and, when winter is over, the general concept of rebirth is celebrated along with the rebirth of the sun.

Spring and harvest festivals are not forgotten and the dead are remembered in the festival of Qing Ming. During the Lantern Festival people make colourful lanterns, small and large, and parade through the streets with them. Another special festival is the birthday of the Jade Emperor.

Since 1000 CE Taoists have identified this emperor with the ruler of heaven, Shang Ti.

A Taoist temple in the wealthy Beverly Hills section above Cebu City in the Philippines.

Reading guide to Taoism

Billington, Ray, *Understanding Eastern Philosophy*, Routledge, London and New York, 1999 edn.

Blofeld, John, *The Secret and the Sublime*: *Taoist Mysteries and Magic*, George Allen & Unwin Ltd, London, 1973.

Cooper, J. C., *Taoism: The Way of the Mystic*, Aquarian Press, Northamptonshire, UK, 1976 edn.

Creel, Herrlee G., *What Is Taoism and Other Studies in Chinese Cultural History*, University of Chicago Press, Chicago and London, 1982 edn.

Deng, Ming Dao, *Chronicles of Tao*: *The Secret Life of a Taoist Master*, HarperCollins, New York, 1993.

Lao-tzu, *Tao Te Ching*: *The Definitive Edition*, Translation and Commentary by Jonathan Star, Tarcher and Penguin, New York, 2003.

Palmer, Martin, *The Elements of Taoism*, Element Books Ltd, Dorset, UK, 1991.

Taylor, Rodney L., *The Confucian Way of Contemplation*, University of South Carolina Press, 1988.

Family and Society

Taoism has long been a philosophical practice which shapes religious practice. It is concerned with the interior life and inner transformation. As such, it has often been at odds with the state system because it places a strong emphasis on personal freedom.

Taoists believe that society and individuals in family units suffer when they live their personal lives in defiance of the *Tao*. Balance and harmony, they believe, are crucially important in society and in personal life. Emphasis is put on healthy living and long life. Oneness with nature is vitally important. Taoism teaches that governments should allow people to grow in a natural way and not, through overly strong prescription, try to force them to be what they are not.

Contemporary Issues

In modern times Taoism has gained a measure of popularity in the West as a wise spiritual path which emphasizes a holistic and nature-based approach to existence.

It has also influenced Western thinking and culture, with the term *Tao* being applied to any number of business and philosophical schools of thought concerned with the maximization of personal success. These draw on aspects of the *Tao* which are undoubtedly helpful to societies and individuals who feel starved of spirituality and need a path that emphasizes balance and health. However, this also represents a challenge for traditional Taoism, as its practitioners see their age-old philosophies reduced to New Age mantras and popular psychology.

Taoism in Asia still exerts a strong influence over popular religion. Many Chinese attend Taoist-inspired festivals and engage in practices such as *feng shui*, which has been popularized and somewhat distorted in Western manifestations. The Chinese continue to worship in Taoist temples, especially in Taiwan.

In Mao Zedong's China it was dangerous for Taoists to practise their faith. Rulers of a new generation are allowing greater freedom. However, a close eye is still kept on all aspects of religious observance and new temples may not be built in China today without specific permission from the authorities.

Shinto

History and Development

Shinto is the indigenous religion of Japan. It has its origins in very ancient times, before the period of written history. The Japanese at this time worshipped deities or powers – *kami* – that lived in natural things and forces.

Size Although nominal adherents could number as many as 100 million, practising Shintoists may number just 4 million.

Founder No single founder of the Shinto religion is known; it emerged from animist origins before written records were kept.

Location Organizing under its present name in the sixth century CE, Shinto is almost exclusively confined to the islands that make up Japan.

Previous page: Six Shinto priests stand before a stairway that leads up to a temple at Toshogu Shrine in Nikko, Japan, c. 1880. It was the final resting place of Ieyasu Tokugawa, the first of the Tokugawa Shoguns.

Above: A crowd at Asakusa Kannon temple watches worshippers carrying a shrine into the temple during the Sanja Festival in Tokyo, Japan.

These deities could be found in trees, mountains, and rivers. They could even be found in the ancestors, in the emperor, and in the sun and the moon. Everything was believed to have a soul or a spirit. The *kami* spirits lived everywhere on the earth. It was a form of nature religion. Relationships between human beings and the *kami* were harmonious. Shrines were established to facilitate the worship and veneration of the spirits.

Shinto means 'the way of the gods' and is applied to a diverse group of religious systems and practices. It emerged as a term in the sixth century CE. The sun goddess assumed a very important role in this early version of Shinto at the head of the hierarchy of gods.

Shinto and Buddhism

Contact with Korea and China strongly influenced the religious development of Japan. Chinese influence, particularly the impact of Buddhism, prompted a great deal of self-reflection within Shinto. Shinto found itself absorbed into Buddhism and was in great danger of losing its own identity. In general, Shinto became the religion of the common people and Buddhism was more prevalent among the upper classes of society. In many areas Shinto and Buddhism became syncretized; it was not unusual for the *kami* to become identified with Buddhas.

Shinto was also strongly influenced by both Taoism and Confucianism. In the eighth century CE, Chinese influence became so great that the Japanese felt obliged to take defensive measures, and began to gather their own writings on Shinto. In addition, the Shinto priests began to formalize and regularize their own religious rituals. Over the centuries various Japanese rulers tried, sometimes forcibly, to limit the impact of Buddhism. However, Buddhism nonetheless exercised a strong influence within Japan. From 1868, the year of the restoration of the monarchy, Emperor Meiji attempted to separate the religious systems from each other. This had three main effects:

◆ State Shinto became identified with the emperor and the government.

◆ A strong cult of the emperor grew up around a major shrine at Ise, dedicated to the sun goddess, Amaterasu.

◆ Practising Shinto was now an expression of patriotism.

For centuries, certainly since the Yamato period, which existed from the fourth to the seventh century CE, the emperor and the imperial family had been a focus of veneration within Shinto. Now the state, the emperor and the sun goddess were all bound together. This continued until after the Second World War, when the semi-divine status of the emperor was disavowed.

Founder and Significant Figures

Shinto has no identifiable single founder. Its rituals and beliefs have evolved over time from the worship of gods and goddesses in ancient Japan. Its origins are in nature worship and spirit worship, and its development is not associated with any one, overarching founder figure.

Branches of Shinto

Shinto has no central doctrine common to all of its branches so practice can vary widely. *State Shinto* was defined by the government as being essentially non-religious in character. It became the national cult, incorporating reverence for the emperor, the imperial family, the household, and the shrines.

Sect Shinto was established by various Shinto sects that were permitted to carry on their practices. It is made up of thirteen groups. Followers meet in halls rather than in shrines. Some groups have very few Shinto features. Sect Shinto groups are governed by independent bodies and appear to have been set up and regularized to bring some order to their organization.

Household Shinto is practised by families and usually includes honouring the ancestors. *Popular Shinto*, also known as *folk Shinto*, is more nebulous; it is made up of a variety of sects and groupings that

177

The torii gate at the Japanese Garden, Brooklyn Botanical Garden, New York City, indicates the presence of a Shinto shrine.

Inside a shrine

Shrines may be situated in sacred locations, near rivers or mountains which have a special significance. Each shrine will have a particular *kami* as a focus. Originally, the natural feature itself will have been the focus of veneration, but gradually a shrine will have grown up around it to give worshippers a place to gather and pay respect. Pilgrimage to shrines is an important feature of Shinto.

The entrance to a shrine will have a ceremonial gate, made up of two upright bars and one across the top. Such gates are known as *torii*. Part of the shrine confines will be given over as an area for purification. Water is kept here so that the face and hands can be washed before prayer. Worshippers can enter the hall of the shrine to engage in corporate prayer, but individual worshippers may also stand outside and pray quietly. The worshipper will alert the *kami* to their presence by pulling on a rope which causes a bell or a clanger to sound. They will also clap their hands.

Offerings of money and food are made. Individuals may visit a shrine for any number of reasons which are personal to themselves. At New Year people visit shrines to seek good fortune for the coming year and to ask for protection from evil spirits.

Festivals

Festivals may be held every year at individual shrines. Popular Shinto encompasses belief in a wide array of superstitious and occult practices which include the minor deities that are to be found in small shrines all over rural Japan. These beliefs have been incorporated into folklore. There is much common ground between popular Shinto and witchcraft which is practised predominantly in the rural communities. Communication with the *kami* may be conducted through mediums. In Shinto, mediums are female.

Shinto festivals draw large numbers of people and are community affairs. Processions are held and they can be very colourful, often made up of decorated floats. During these festivals, offerings are made to the *kami*.

Family and Society

The idea of the group is very important within Shinto and people must always act with the needs of the whole community in mind. This belief inspires devotion to workplaces, school communities, and family. The self should always come last.

The very close identification of Shinto with the nation of Japan itself gives it a highly patriotic and nationalistic character. It therefore has a certain exclusive nature. Paradoxically, however, it has borrowed from other faiths, particularly Buddhism. It is sustained by its unique relationship with the Japanese people and so is likely to continue its role as a national unifier for many generations to come.

Contemporary Issues

Shinto developed in a Japan that was pre-modern and intensely agricultural. A religion so closely tied to the rhythms of rural life is bound to be challenged by the evolution of Japan into a highly industrialized and urbanized society. Shinto leaders are trying to formulate an approach which will make Shinto relevant in such a culture. The rise of what are called 'new religions' is also greatly challenging the traditional role of Shinto.

Reading guide to Shinto

Mullins, Mark; Shimazono, Susumu & Swanson, Paul L., ed., *Religion and Society in Modern Japan: Selected Readings,* Asian Humanities Press, Berkeley, California, USA, 1993.

Nelson, John K., *A Year in the Life of a Shinto Shrine,* University of Washington Press, 1996.

Reader, Ian, *Religion in Contemporary Japan,* MacMillan Press Ltd, Hampshire and London, 1991.

Reader, Ian; Andreasen, Esben & Stefansson, Finn, *Japanese Religions Past and Present,* Japan Library, Sandgate, Folkestone, Kent, UK, 1993.

Ross, Floyd Hiatt, *Shinto: The Way of Japan,* Greenwood Press, Connecticut, USA, 1983 edn.

Shimazono, Susumu, *From Salvation to Spirituality: Popular Religious Movements in Modern Japan,* Transpacific Press, Melbourne, 2004.

Tanabe, George Joji, ed., *Religions of Japan in Practice,* Princeton Readings in Religion, Princeton University Press, Princeton, New Jersey, USA, 1999.

Yusa, Michiko, *Japanese Religions,* Routledge, London, 2002.

Notes

Chapter 1   Christiantity
1. See Martin, Hugh, *The Beatitudes,* Camelot Press, London, 1952.

Note that Matthew writes of eight beatitudes – nine if 'Blessed are you when people insult you...' is included. However, the possible ninth beatitude is often regarded as an extension of the eighth, so there is some debate as to the exact number of beatitudes that Matthew lists.

2. See Bruce, F. F., *Second Thoughts on the Dead Sea Scrolls,* Paternoster Press, Exeter, 1979, fourth edn.; Kee, Howard Clark, *What Can We Know About Jesus?,* Cambridge University Press, Cambridge, 1990; Fitzmeyer, Joseph A., *Responses to 101 Questions on the Dead Sea Scrolls,* Geoffrey Chapman, London, 1992.

3. See Harrington, Daniel J., S. J., *Invitation to the Apocrypha,* William B. Eerdmans, Michigan/Cambridge, UK, 1999.

Chapter 2   Judaism
1. See Jacobs, Louis, *The Oxford Concise Companion to the Jewish Religion,* Oxford University Press, Oxford, 1999; Neusner, Jacob, *Judaism: An Introduction,* Penguin Books, London, 2002.

2. See Neusner, Jacob, *Judaism: An Introduction,* Penguin Books, London, 2002, pp. 77–80.

Chapter 3   Islam
1. See Matthews, Warren, *World Religions,* West Publishing Company, St Paul, MN, 1991, pp. 375–76.

2. See Chapman, Colin, *Islam and the West: Conflict, Co-existence or Conversion,* Paternoster Press, Carlisle, UK, 1998, pp. 57–80; Ernst, Carl W., *Rethinking Islam in the Contemporary World,* Edinburgh University Press, Edinburgh, 2004.

Chapter 4   Zoroastrianism
1. Taken from Zaehner, R. C., *The Teachings of the Magi,* Sheldon Press, London, 1975, used by permission of SPCK.

2. See Boyce, Mary, *Zoroastrians: Their Religious Beliefs and Practices,* Routledge and Kegan Paul, London, 1979; Zaehner, R. C., *The Dawn and Twilight of Zoroastrianism,* Weidenfield and Nicolson, London, 1961; Zaehner, R. C., *The Teachings of the Magi,* George Allen and Unwin Ltd, London, 1975.

Chapter 5   Bahá'í
1. See Miller, William McElwee, *What is the Bahá'í Faith?,* William B. Eerdmans, Michigan, 1974.

2. See Ferraby, John, *All Things Made New: An Introduction to the Bahá'í Faith,* Bahá'í Publishing Trust, London, 1987 edn.

Chapter 6   Hinduism
1. Information taken from Klostermaier, Klaus K., *A Short Introduction to Hinduism,* Oneworld Publications, Oxford, 2005.

2. See Kinsley, D. R., *Hinduism: A Cultural Perspective,* Prentice-Hall, New Jersey, 1982.

Chapter 7   Jainism
1. See Dundas, Paul, *The Jains,* Routledge, London, 1992.

2. See Cort, John E., *Jains in the World: Religious Values and Ideology in India*, Oxford University Press, New York, 2001.

Chapter 8 Sikhism

1. See Singh, Nikky-Guninder Kaur, *Sikhism: World Religions*, Facts on File, New York, 1993; Oxtoby, Willard G., ed., *World Religions: Eastern Traditions*, Oxford University Press, Ontario, Canada, 1996.

s. See Oxtoby, Willard G., ed., *World Religions: Eastern Traditions*, Oxford University Press, Ontario, Canada, 1996.

Chapter 9 Buddhism

1. See Harvey, Peter, *An Introduction to Buddhism: Teachings, History and Practices*, Cambridge University Press, Cambridge, 1990.

2. See Harris, Elizabeth J., *What Buddhists Believe*, Oneworld Publications, Oxford, 2001.

Chapter 10 Confucianism

1. See Billington, Ray, *Understanding Eastern Philosophy*, Routledge, London, 1999 edn.

Chapter 11 Taoism

1. See Billington, Ray; *Understanding Eastern Philosophy*, Routledge, London, 1999 edn.; Creel, Herrlee G., *What Is Taoism and Other Studies in Chinese Cultural History*, University of Chicago Press, Chicago and London, 1982 edn.; Lao-tzu, *Tao Te Ching: The Definitive Edition*, Translation and Commentary by Jonathan Star, Tarcher and Penguin, New York, 2003.

Chapter 12 Shinto

1. See Reader, Ian, *Religion in Contemporary Japan*, Macmillan Press Ltd, Hampshire and London, 1991.

Bibliography

General reading

Beckerlegge, Gwilym, ed., *The World Religions Reader*, Routledge, London, 2001, second edn.

Cole, W. Owen & Morgan, Peggy, *Six Religions in the Twenty-First Century*, Stanley Thornes, Cheltenham, UK, 2000.

Esposito et al, ed., *World Religions Today*, Oxford University Press, New York, 2006.

Jurgensmeyer, Mark, ed., *The Oxford Handbook of Global Religions*, Oxford University Press, 2006.

Matthews, Warren, *World Religions*, West Publishing Company, Saint Paul, Minnesota, 1991.

Morgan, Peggy & Lawton, Clive, ed., *Ethical Issues in Six Religious Traditions*, Edinburgh University Press, Edinburgh, 1996.

Oxtoby, Willard, ed., *World Religions: Eastern Traditions*, Oxford University Press, Ontario, 1996.

Oxtoby, Willard, ed., *World Religions: Western Traditions*, Oxford University Press, Ontario, 1996.

Partridge, Christopher, ed., *The New Lion Handbook to the World's Religions*, Lion, Oxford, 2005, third edn.

Smart, Ninian, *The World's Religions*, Cambridge University Press, Cambridge, 1998, second edn.

Woodhead, Linda et al, ed., *Religions in the Modern World*, Routledge, London, 2002.

Index

Acknowledgments

Corbis: p. 22bl Alessandra Benedetti; p. 25 Joe Cornish/Arcaid; p. 44 Philippe Lissac /Godong; p. 69tl Bernard Bisson/Sygma; p. 69r Rob Howard; p. 93 Jon Hicks; p. 96 Chris Rainier; p. 99 John Van Hasselt; p. 108 Martin Harvey; pp. 109, 176 Bob Krist; p. 129r Michele Falzone/JAI; p. 134 Kapoor Baldev/Sygma; p. 138 Annie Griffiths Belt; p. 143 Alison Wright; p. 145 Marco Bulgarelli; p. 153 So Hing-Keung; p. 155 Kazuyoshi Nomachi; p. 157 Angelo Cavalli; p. 160 Luca Tettoni; p. 163 Peter M. Wilson; p. 169 Liu Liqun; p. 173 Paul A. Souders; p. 175 Michael Maslan Historic Photographs; p. 179 Dallas and John Heaton/Free Agents p. 180 Lee Snider/Photo Images

Kate and Matt Kirkpatrick: pp. 19, 40tr, 66-67, 104, 106, 107

Lion Hudson: p. 41 (inset and background)

Picture research by Zooid Pictures Ltd: pp. 8 Sebastian Scheiner/Press Association Images, 11 akg-images, 12 Bill Bachmann/Alamy, 13 Bill Bachmann/Alamy, 14 Santa Maria della Grazie, Milan, Italy/Bridgeman Art Library, 15 Cameraphoto/akg-images, 16 The London Art Archive/Alamy, 17 akg-images, 22t P Deliss/ Godong/Corbis UK Ltd., 24 Alexander Nemenov/ AFP/Getty Images, 27 John Morrison/Alamy, 28 Robert Nickelsberg/Getty Images, 30 Erich Lessing/akg-images, 32 Robert Atanasovski/ AFP/Getty Images, 33 The Art Archive/Corbis UK Ltd., 34 Noah Seelam/AFP/Getty Images, 36 Bill Bachmann/Alamy, 38 akg-images, 39 akg-images, 40l North Wind Picture Archives/Alamy, 42 akg-images, 43 akg-images, 45 Hanan Isachar/ Corbis UK Ltd., 47 Olszanka/Rex Features, 48 Hunt Add E (R)/The Bodleian Library/Art Archive, 49 Leland Bobbè/Corbis UK Ltd., 52 Andy Aitchison/Corbis UK Ltd., 53 Robert Wallis/Corbis UK Ltd., 55 Erich Lessing/ akg-images, 57 Daniel Berehulak/Getty Images, 60 Mohammed Sawaf/AFP/Getty Images, 61 Erich Lessing/akg-images, 63 Sipa Press/Rex Features, 66 Kazuyoshi Nomachi/Corbis UK Ltd., 72 Robert Harding Picture Library Ltd/ Alamy, 73 Robert Harding Picture Library Ltd/ Alamy, 74 Reza/Getty Images, 77 Atta Kenare/ AFP/Getty Images, 79 Lindsay Hebberd/Corbis UK Ltd., 80 Raheb Homavandi/Reuters/Corbis UK Ltd., 81 Patrick Ward/Alamy, 83 Bahá'í World Centre archives/Bahá'í International Community, 85 Bahá'í International Community, 86 Bahá'í International Community, 87 Bahá'í World Centre archives/Bahá'í International Community, 88 Craig Lovell/Corbis UK Ltd., 90 Commercial Appeal/Landov/Press Association Images, 91 Bahá'í International Community, 93 Louise Batalla Duran/Alamy, 101 The British Library/Heritage Images, 102 Atlantide Phototravel/Corbis UK Ltd., 103 British Library/akg-images, 112 Craig Lovell/ Eagle Visions Photography/Alamy, 113 Monique Pietri/akg-images, 114 Craig Lovell/Eagle Visions Photography/Alamy, 116 Jagadeesh Nv/Reuters/Corbis UK Ltd., 117 Sebastian D'Souza/AFP/Getty Images, 118 Gautam Singh/ Press Association Images, 120 Shutterstock, 121 Louise Batalla Duran/Alamy, 123 G & R Maschmeyer/Pacific Stock/Photolibrary Group, 124 Gautam Singh/Press Association Images, 125 Jayesh Bhagat/iStockphoto, 127 Yvan Travert/akg-images, 128/129 Yvan Travert/ akg-images, 132 World Religions Photo Library/ Alamy, 133 World Religions Photo Library/ Alamy, 136 Vinicius Valle/Alamy, 140 Peter MacDiarmid/Rex Features, 141 Sylvan Barnet and William Burto Collection/Art Archive,

146/147 Liu Yu/Redlink/Corbis UK Ltd., 148 Sylvan Barnet and William Burto Collection/Art Archive, 150 Ullstein Bild/akg-images, 159 The Granger Collection/TopFoto, 161 The Granger Collection/TopFoto, 164/165 Michael Kappeler/AFP/Getty Images, 167 Stapleton Historical Collection/Heritage Images, 170 Uniphoto Press International/Ancient Art & Architecture Collection